DONALD
TRUMP
VS.
KIM
JONG-UN

A SPIRITUAL BATTLE
BETWEEN TWO
LEADERS

RYUHO OKAWA

HS PRESS

Contents

✑ PROLOGUE ✑

Simulation of a War Outbreak

✑ CHAPTER ONE ✑

Spiritual Interview with the Guardian Spirit of Kim Jong-un

The insane strategies of a young dictator

Spiritual Interview with the Guardian Spirit of Donald Trump

The contents of hard-line measures that remind us of the Cuban Missile Crisis

Trump is Attempting to Pull Off An Amazing Move

Chapter 2 is the transcript of the spiritual interview with the guardian spirit of Donald Trump that was conducted in English. Other chapters are English translations of what were originally conducted in Japanese.

These spiritual messages were channeled through Ryuho Okawa by his extraordinary spiritual power. For the mechanism behind spiritual messages, see end section.

Preface

The North Korean nuclear development and missile firing problem is approaching its final stage. On the afternoon of August 29, the day when a North Korean ballistic missile flew over the Japanese archipelago and caused pandemonium on the ground, I held an urgent interview with the guardian spirits of both Mr. Kim Jong-un and Mr. Trump.

I will save the details of those interviews for the main portion of this book, but I will say here that while Mr. Kim Jong-un is aiming for a technical knockout, Mr. Trump is planning on throwing North Korea completely out of the ring.

If we accept that North Korea is a nuclear power as an established fact, the future of both Japan and the U.S. will be in danger and the entire world will enter an era of multi-polarization and wars for hegemony.

As for me, my only advice for North Korea is to immediately stop missile and nuclear development and agree to a bloodless surrender. To accept defeat gracefully in order to protect the citizens is also a necessary quality of a country's ruler.

Ryuho Okawa
Founder and CEO of Happy Science Group
August 30, 2017

Prologue

Simulation of a War Outbreak

On the morning of August 29, An "air-raid alarm" rung out in East Japan

RYUHO OKAWA

Today is August 29 [of 2017], and from around 8:00 in the morning I had planned to proofread a manuscript of an English spiritual interview with Malcolm X, a black leader who was assassinated [see, *Malcolm X no Reigen* (literally, Spiritual Interview with Malcolm X) (Tokyo: IRH Press, 2017)].

However, when I set about to start that work, my secretary came up and said, "Master, you need to watch the television right now." So, I turned on the television only to see that every news station was saying, "A missile has been launched from North Korea."

On August 26, North Korea had already launched a missile which dropped in the Sea of Japan. This time around, the missile flew over Tsugaru Strait and Hokkaido and dropped into the Pacific Ocean about 1,000 kilometers away from Cape Erimo. The maximum altitude was about 550 kilometers and it apparently flew a distance of approximately 2,700 kilometers. I believe this is the way to fire a missile over a long distance at the standard altitude.

We did not hear this where I was, but this time around, an alarm called "J ALERT" apparently rang several times in the morning from the Ibaraki Prefecture area to the Hokkaido area.

Looking at the reports from the affected areas, it was supposedly an air-raid alarm that meant something along the lines of, "A missile just passed over." The bullet trains were also stopped, and I imagine East Japan was in a state of alarm.

I do not know if the Prime Minister's Official Residence was on standby or not, but they were active from relatively early in the morning. If the missiles had been launched while Prime Minister Abe was playing golf, I believe that would have been dangerous in a political meaning.

Kim Jong-un had resisted firing any missiles for about one month, so American President Trump had said he made a very wise decision, and praised him a bit. However, three days later, North Korea went ahead and launched three missiles.

And right now, a hurricane is attacking the U.S. with a massive amount of damage occurring centered in the Texas area, so President Trump is in the position of having to observe what is going on with that. It is within that environment that North Korea is doing this sort of thing again.

Japan fell completely for
Kim Jong-un's diversionary tactic

RYUHO OKAWA

North Korea recently said, "We are preparing to shoot four missiles toward the area around the U.S. territory of Guam." They were uncharacteristically specific, saying, "Those missiles will pass over Shimane, Hiroshima, and Kochi Prefectures in Japan as they head toward Guam."

Because of this, Japan had to also deploy its very limited number of PAC-3 missile interceptors to Chugoku and Shikoku regions [in western Japan], and right as Japan was setting those in place, North Korean missiles were shot toward the Hokkaido and Aomori Prefecture areas instead.

This was a diversionary tactic. I had thought as much. I felt, "They would not say, 'We are going to aim it here,' and then actually aim it at that same place. That man [Kim Jong-un] is not so 'simple-minded' as to aim it right where we are on alert. He is a much more challenging type of individual, so he will most likely say, 'I am going to aim it there,' and then aim it at an entirely different place."

When North Korea said, "We are going to fire toward Guam," I immediately thought, "They are probably going to aim at some other place like Alaska, the West Coast, or Hawaii, which are all part of the U.S." North Korea is fully aware of Japan's weak point of not having very many PAC-3 units, and since the interceptor missiles only fly about 20 to 30 kilometers, the units must be brought close to the area where the missiles are likely to hit.

The missile payload could also be Chemical or biological weaponry

RYUHO OKAWA

This time around, the North Korean missile that was shot apparently divided up into three parts and flew over the Tsugaru Strait before landing in the water. Because the missile separated into three parts, it is being said that they were probably Hwasong-12 type missiles. It is thought that there is a high likelihood that this was a new type of missile tested, so that it can be aimed toward Guam.

Japan's PAC-3 missiles work by firing two against a single missile, so this means that if an enemy drops a warhead in three separate locations, one location will not be covered. If they do not fire another interceptor missile, they will not be able to cover all three warheads. Those who are in charge of defense [of Japan] might think, "North Korea must have tried to frighten us by letting the missile separate into several parts."

If missiles were to break apart and fall in separate locations around Hokkaido or Northeast Japan like Aomori, there could be hazardous substance inside the missiles, so I think that is very frightening.

Japanese people are only worried about nuclear weapons, but the missile warheads do not necessarily have to be limited to nuclear weapons. North Korea possesses chemical and biological weaponry as well.

If we are attacked by chemical or biological weaponry, then even if we are able to shoot down the missile, while we would know that it is not a nuclear missile, we would not be able to tell it apart from a conventional missile immediately. If the missile delivers bacteriological weaponry [biological weaponry], we would not be able to know until a while later. In the case of chemical weaponry, there is no way to immediately verify the causal relationship to the damage that would occur.

Thus, we cannot completely tell what exactly would happen if a part of a missile were to fall.

Even Aum Shinrikyo [a cult in Japan] was able to develop sarin and planned on scattering it from the sky above. North Korea has developed this kind of thing at a national level, so it is entirely possible that they have something more of a weapon than what Aum Shinrikyo had.

It is no overstatement to say that They have already engaged in an act of war

RYUHO OKAWA

North Korea said, "We are going to fire missiles at the Guam area," and American President Trump said, "If they do that, they will be met with fire and fury." In such a situation, North Korea made such kind of feint.

Furthermore, they chose to do it at a time when the U.S. was busy dealing with a hurricane. Their news was basically covering the hurricane only. For Japan, ultimately we are "being protected by the U.S." We cannot do anything on our own. Because of that, when the U.S. is busy dealing with a hurricane and sort of saying, "Wait a minute here," the sense of impending doom heightens.

This time around, at the very least, something similar to a citywide air-raid alarm broadcast was sent out, telling everyone things like, "A missile was fired," "The missile is passing by," and "The missile passed over." Also, at Tokyo Station an announcement was broadcast saying, "A missile was fired, so please take shelter within your train or in the waiting room." In a sense, I do not think it is an overstatement to say, "They have already engaged in an act of war."

Due to all of this, and because it has been a while since our last spiritual interview with Kim Jong-un's guardian spirit [see *Kiki no Naka no Kitachosen Kim Jong-un no Shugorei*

Reigen (literally, North Korea in Crisis: A Spiritual Interview with the Guardian Spirit of Kim Jong-un)(Tokyo: IRH Press, 2017)], I would like to conduct a spiritual interview with his guardian spirit today.

I do not know if he will make his true feelings and thoughts clear to us or not, but since he is the kind of person who talks a lot, he might divulge his true thoughts today. However, there is also a possibility that we will be tricked and lied to, and we could end up being used by him, so I want our interviewers to be shrewd in terms of that.

There is also a chance that he might get puffed up with pride and accidentally spill the beans, so my feeling is that I would like to let him say whatever he feels like saying as much as possible without holding any preconceptions.

Will President Trump aim for an assassination of Kim Jong-un and simultaneously attack Militarily as well?

RYUHO OKAWA

Regarding President Trump, during the previous spiritual interview with his guardian spirit [recorded on April 25, 2017], we asked his guardian spirit, "What do you plan to do?" The response was basically, "Things like military attack schedules are top-secret, so I cannot make that information public. And I could never agree to give a spiritual message about that either. If I speak about those things, the situation could change." So, we did not dig deep into that topic then.

However, now that we are at this stage, we can assume that he has concrete plans, so we have to have him tell us something. For one thing, Japan would be at a significant loss if it were left out in the cold, being an ally of the U.S. So, I want him to tell us a little bit more about what he is thinking.

What I think will happen is, the U.S. will go ahead and aim for an assassination at a time when Kim Jong-un absolutely has to appear in a public setting. That is my sincere prediction. And since there is always the chance that an assassination attempt might not succeed, they may also engage in a diversionary attack simultaneously. If it were me, that is what I would plan.

This is the most effective course of action. For example, when former President Obama was in office, he mounted a night attack on the person of Osama bin Laden. However, there is talk of Kim Jong-un having about 50 or 60 doubles [as already cited, see "North Korea in Crisis: A Spiritual Interview with the Guardian Spirit of Kim Jong-un"], so if the wrong person is targeted, the plan might go up in smoke.

If Kim Jong-un is put on alert by that and is thus able to escape, what would happen then? North Korea is said to have a stronghold 150 meters below ground, so he might burrow down there and give orders from there. This place is believed to withstand nuclear attacks as well, so I imagine that he can continue fighting by giving orders from there, meaning that the resultant war damage would be even more immense.

South Korea underestimates the threat and Japan is too ignorant of the crisis

RYUHO OKAWA

The current president of South Korea [Moon Jae-in] is also a problem. Why the Korean people would ever want to choose an appeaser for their president in these times is beyond me.

The policy of appeasement was the reason why Hitler grew stronger and World War II broke out. Right now, that exact sort of person who underestimates the threat is taking the chair in South Korea. The South Korean president is the type of person who could even find himself immediately on the wrong side if not pushed by the U.S., so this is also something that may be very dangerous.

Moreover, South Korea is the kind of nation that puts a statue of a military comfort woman on the front seat of its town bus just when the Japanese-Korean alliance needs to be strengthened. I cannot help but feel like telling them that they're on their own. In that sense, there is a question as to whether Japan and South Korea can harmonize in a comprehensive way.

Also, regarding Japan as well, I just cannot help feeling that people are much too ignorant of the crisis.

Today, there was a television report covering Hokkaido and Tohoku region, where sirens rang out. The citizens and farmers who were interviewed all smiled broadly and said things like, "Shooting off a missile all of a sudden like that sure is concerning."

Aide to Master [Shio Okawa] saw that and got angry saying, "They shouldn't show such broad smiles!" The wrong signal could be sent and people over there could think the Japanese people look happy about North Korea shooting missiles.

As expected, Seoul's special correspondent reported on this with a scowl to prevent North Korea from misunderstanding their expressions. Japanese people have a habit of speaking in an upbeat, positive manner in these kinds of instances, so we need to be careful of this sort of thing. We have to clearly show that we are angry about it.

In any case, the tension might be increasing quite a bit in this way. It seems like we are completely in a game of chicken, where it is a race to see which side would attack first. If an actual war breaks out, I do not think North Korea has any chance of winning against the U.S. However, depending on the way North Korea mounts a surprise attack, there is also a chance that the U.S. forces could undergo massive damages.

For example, if they establish a goal to shoot through the deck of an aircraft carrier and suddenly strike with the intent of carrying out a surprise attack, they could actually succeed in that. So, the U.S. could actually take damage in that sense. Or, North Korea could also aim for a U.S. base and inflict damage there. In this way, we can consider that there might be damage to be suffered from a surprise attack.

Furthermore, depending on the way they fight, there is also a danger of Japan and South Korea suffering massive amounts of damage.

"Winning a war but still suffering immense damages" is a possible case. If Kim Jong-un is considering a plan to bring everyone down with him, thinking, "If I am going to die, you all have to die with me," and tries to bring as many people as he can along to Hell, that would be very troublesome. So, I really think the U.S. should deliberate on how the fight could unfold.

Summoning the guardian spirit of Kim Jong-un, The third leader of North Korea, To listen to his true feelings

RYUHO OKAWA

With that being said, I want the interviewers today to try their best. There is no other place that can conduct this kind of investigation. Other places will not be able to capture him and force him to talk. I'm sure the U.S. would want to do that if they could, but since they cannot pour water on him and make him confess like they did at detention facilities in Guantanamo, the only other way is to just peek at what is inside his mind through his guardian spirit. I want to frankly hear what he is thinking with the most neutral stance possible.

Secondly, I want to hear what President Trump plans on doing. OK, let's get started.

JIRO AYAORI

We're ready.

RYUHO OKAWA

I'd like to summon the guardian spirit of Kim Jong-un, the third leader of North Korea. I'd like to hear about his condition and most recent state of mind and thoughts.

Oh, the guardian spirit of Kim Jong-un, leader of North Korea.

I'm sorry for summoning you so many times, but please share what's on your mind at Happy Science General Headquarters.

Chapter One

Spiritual Interview with the Guardian Spirit of Kim Jong-un

The insane strategies of a young dictator

Recorded August 29, 2017
Happy Science General Headquarters,
Japan

Kim Jong-un (1983? - Present)

The third supreme leader of North Korea. The third son of previous General Secretary Kim Jong-il, he inherited the status of supreme leader after Kim Jong-il died in December 2011. Currently, he holds the titles of Chairman of the Workers' Party of Korea, Chairman of the State Affairs Commission of DPRK, and the Supreme Commander of the Korean People's Army, and so on.

Interviewers from Happy Science[*]:

Jiro Ayaori
Managing Director
Chief Editor of *The Liberty*
Lecturer of Happy Science University

Yuki Oikawa
Director of Foreign Affairs
Happiness Realization Party

Kazuhiro Ichikawa
Senior Managing Director
Chief Director of International Headquarters

The opinions of the spirit do not necessarily reflect those of Happy Science Group.

---

[*] The interviewer's professional title represents the position at the time of the interview.

"Right now, the world is revolving around me,"
Boasts the guardian spirit of Kim Jong-un

KIM JONG-UN'S GUARDIAN SPIRIT

[*Slaps the chair's armrest with right hand.*] Hmm.

JIRO AYAORI

Hello.

KIM JONG-UN'S G.S.

[*Slaps the chair's armrest with both hands.*] Yes.

AYAORI

Everyone in the world is now paying attention to Chairman Kim.

KIM JONG-UN'S G.S.

Well yes, it is the truth that I am moving this world.

AYAORI

Yes, that is certainly true.

KIM JONG-UN'S G.S.

Yes. The world is revolving around me. I am currently the North Pole.

AYAORI

The North Pole?

KIM JONG-UN'S G.S.

Yes, similar to the North Pole, I am at the center, and the world is what is revolving. It is circling around me.

AYAORI

I understand, that is certainly true. Precisely, the world's most viewed news is today's [August 29, 2017] missile launch.

KIM JONG-UN'S G.S.

Do you now understand how great I am? Even a little? Hahaha [*laughs*].

AYAORI

Hmm, well I'm not sure if you are great.

Plans for attacking Japan or South Korea Instead of America

KIM JONG-UN'S G.S.

Japan is hopeless. Do you understand how easy it is to get rid of Mr. Abe? Hah. I can even hit Yamaguchi. Hmph!

AYAORI

Yamaguchi?

KIM JONG-UN'S G.S.

Yes. As the prime minister, he'll be disgraced if his hometown [Yamaguchi Prefecture] is ruined. He can't even protect his own hometown. Hahaha [*laughs*].

AYAORI

I understand. So, are you thinking about attacking the Japanese mainland?

KIM JONG-UN'S G.S.

Of course, it's more efficient to attack Japan or South Korea. If we fight America, we will first suffer damages. If we attack Japan or South Korea, at the very least, the damages that we will suffer will be delayed a little bit. And we will be able to gain some achievements. Isn't that so?

AYAORI

Hmm... However, if this happens, America will be first to move, right?

KIM JONG-UN'S G.S.

I wonder? Hmm... is that really so? Is it enough reason for

America to take action after only having a missile hit Mr. Abe's parents' home?

AYAORI
Well yes, it is.

KIM JONG-UN'S G.S.
Of course, they have to debate it at the United Nations.

AYAORI
Well, America is not that easygoing.

KIM JONG-UN'S G.S.
The damage won't be large. It'll only burn up the area surrounding Mr. Abe's parents' home.

The plan was to aim for another location After claiming to target Guam

AYAORI
Regarding today's talk, there has been increased tension after your mentioning of firing four missiles into Guam.

KIM JONG-UN'S G.S.
Well we would fire. We are prepared.

AYAORI

President Trump has said that they [North Korea] will be "met with fire and fury like the world has never seen." At that point, you had put off the plan, and had taken away the idea of firing missiles into Guam for a moment. Then, a few days ago, [August 26, 2017], you fired one into the Sea of Japan, and today, another one that flew over the Japanese mainland, which has not happened since 2009. This is...

KIM JONG-UN'S G.S.

Well, it was proven that Japan cannot shoot it down. As I thought, they did not destroy it. Hehe [*laughs*]. You can't shoot it down, can you?

AYAORI

Well, you could say so. Since a portion of the PAC-3 had moved to western Japan.*

KIM JONG-UN'S G.S.

This was something that never crossed your mind, right? That's why you are all too trusting. I say that "it's going to fly over this area" and you actually wait in that location. You're like a child. Ahahaha [*laughs*].

---

* PAC-3 was deployed from the Japan Air Self-Defense Force's bases in Gifu, Mie and Shiga Prefectures to Japan Ground Self-Defense Force's bases in Shimane, Hiroshima, Ehime, and Kochi Prefectures.

AYAORI

That was originally part of the plan, right? After the PAC-3 was moved, you targeted the north.

KIM JONG-UN'S G.S.

Well, if I say, "This is where I will shoot" and both Japan and America are waiting there to shoot it down, and are successful, they would both report to the world how they "successfully shot down the missile." Then, North Korea will look foolish. We aren't stupid enough to not notice that.

Get somebody who's a bit more intelligent. You have already lost in the battle of intellect. In a war, before the actual battle, there is a battle of intellect. You must understand that there are differences in intellect between us. You are dealing with a genius. Do you understand?

Kim Jong-un's aim is to cause a turmoil through A mental war by the use of words

AYAORI

One thing we can expect to happen is, there is now a greater chance that America will decide to take military action.

KIM JONG-UN'S G.S.

At least Obama... Not Obama, not him. He's dead. No, he didn't die, he just quit.

What Trump did when I said I would attack Guam was that he became worried that they would lose tourists. So, he said something to the effect of, "This will make Guam world-famous and surely boost tourism by 110%." The fact that he felt the need to play them up shows that it agitated him.

AYAORI

I see.

KIM JONG-UN'S G.S.

Of course, they might lose tourists, it's not safe. So, now we know for a fact that we can cause a turmoil through a psychological war. What do you think would happen if we say that our next aim is Trump Tower? That would be great fun [*laughs*]. We don't even have to shoot. Words alone will do the job. All we need to do is to say that we are confident we can accurately target Trump Tower.

AYAORI

You mean the one in New York?

KIM JONG-UN'S G.S.

Yeah, exactly. What do you think would happen if we announced that we are confident that our new missile can target Trump Tower within a seven-meter margin of error? The Happy Science General Headquarters is too small, so we might miss it, but we could hit something the size of Trump Tower.

The police can't protect it. The police costs are astronomical, right? Even Tiffany is in the red due to the protection around Trump Tower. So, in order to save Tiffany we should quickly destroy Trump Tower.

AYAORI

At any rate, though, it's not long till America makes a final decision.

KIM JONG-UN'S G.S.

So, if we say we are targeting Trump Tower, then all of the residents are sure to begin evacuating. Tiffany would probably end up closing its doors and announce a one-year shutdown.

AYAORI

But the fact that America might decide to take military action...

KIM JONG-UN'S G.S.

A physical warfare isn't the only kind of war. A psychological war is also a type of warfare. So, it's started...

AYAORI

So, from your standpoint, does it mean that you are already at war? Is that how you see it?

KIM JONG-UN'S G.S.

Hmm. What I mean is, not only Trump Tower, but what's that thing in Florida? A vacation house or is it a hotel? He owns something there, right? The place where he had lunch with Xi Jinping. You know?

AYAORI

You mean Mar-a-Lago.

KIM JONG-UN'S G.S.

If we just verbally say that we can "hit" his hotel in Florida, it would get zero customers.

AYAORI

I see.

KIM JONG-UN'S G.S.

Hahahaha.

AYAORI

So, you're saying that a war has already begun.

KIM JONG-UN'S G.S.

It has, verbally. Or at least mentally, from long time ago.

AYAORI

I see.

Kim Jong-un's G.S. keeps mocking the practice of Bombing runs conducted during The U.S.-South Korea joint military exercises

KIM JONG-UN'S G.S.

I mean, the U.S. and South Korea are conducting military exercises even though we've been launching missiles and telling them to stay away, so it's important to show that we are prepared to retaliate. That's why I launched a missile directly over Japan. Did you hear what they did during their military exercises? Rather than attacking back, they were reporting about how they managed to drop eight tons of explosives [one ton of bomb 8 times] and hit the target in a field in South Korea. Can't you see how chicken-hearted they are? I mean, if they're going to drop bombs, drop them in Pyongyang.

AYAORI

Wow... Are you saying they can?

KIM JONG-UN'S G.S.

I mean, they... [*laughs*]. The fact that the joint forces of the U.S. and South Korea are announcing how they successfully hit the targets inside South Korea with eight tons of explosives, and thinking that they could stand against us, means they have already lost. They are already defeated.

AYAORI

I see. So, the state of the war...

KIM JONG-UN'S G.S.

Our shot already flew over Japan. So, we could hit Japan. We could even shoot over it, to the other side of Japan, and target anywhere in America. We might even suddenly attack someplace that has close relations with America. They would be completely defenseless. These countries would suffer for having such a close relationship with America.

AYAORI

So, conversely, from your point of view, you're wondering why they didn't bomb Pyongyang?

KIM JONG-UN'S G.S.

I don't get it. I would have done it a long time ago.

AYAORI

I see.

KIM JONG-UN'S G.S.

You think saying that you successfully hit targets inside South Korea with eight tons of explosives is going to scare us? Don't be stupid.

AYAORI

Then a situation where America and South Korea both attack...

KIM JONG-UN'S G.S.

Don't be stupid. They should just drop eight tons [of bombs] on Pyongyang. We would then attack Seoul with a barrage from 550 pieces of artillery.

"America is, after all, a bureaucratic country And the soldiers are all bureaucrats"

AYAORI

But America is considering countermeasures to that, and they are devising a plan to clear it all away in one fell swoop.

KIM JONG-UN'S G.S.

If only they could. But we are more intelligent than them.

AYAORI

Is that so?

KIM JONG-UN'S G.S.

We just always end up being one step ahead of them.

AYAORI

Oh, I see.

KIM JONG-UN'S G.S.

They're just stupid. America claims to be a country of freedom and meritocratic, but they are, after all, bureaucratic. Also, the soldiers are bureaucrats. They've only threatened countries that don't fight, so when a country that is willing to fight shows up, it ends up being just like Japan's civil war period. Only someone who has participated in an actual war can fight against me. That's why I'm telling you to bring someone like Yukimura Sanada [a brave Japanese military commander who is said to have daringly challenged Ieyasu Tokugawa]. If not, they wouldn't be able to imagine what I plan to do.

AYAORI

Then, would you teach us a part of your genius mind? America is planning to wipe out all of North Korea's artillery pieces installed along the border between North and South Koreas in one fell swoop. What do you plan to do in response?

KIM JONG-UN'S G.S.

Even when we've done nothing? Nothing to wiping us out all at once? Do you really think they could wipe us out all at once even when we haven't made our attack?

AYAORI

There is a possibility that they will conduct a preemptive attack, right?

KIM JONG-UN'S G.S.

That's just racism. That would be a racist attack by white people on people of color. Just like, "No more Hiroshima or Nagasaki," its "No more Pyongyang." It's unacceptable to attack us when we haven't made our attack.

AYAORI

That's a different issue. It has nothing to do with white supremacy.

"We are not a democracy, so our attacks Will launch just seconds after I give the order"

KIM JONG-UN'S G.S.

There is no way that they could destroy all of our artillery when we haven't done anything. This should be discussed at the U.S. Congress while the world watches.

AYAORI

No, no. Didn't you say that it's already in a state of war? This is exactly what you said.

KIM JONG-UN'S G.S.

Yeah, but the Congress hasn't approved it yet. Sometimes a war is declared after it has already begun, but in a democracy, there are procedures...

AYAORI

Right. But if the American president decides to do it, it can be done.

KIM JONG-UN'S G.S.

Democracy is, I'll tell you... The procedure is important in a democracy. You have to follow the procedure...

AYAORI

[*Smiles wryly.*] I don't want to be lectured on that by someone like you.

KIM JONG-UN'S G.S.

Maybe you don't. But we are not a democracy.

AYAORI

[*Smiles wryly.*]

KIM JONG-UN'S G.S.

We are a theocracy of god. And I am the god. As soon as I give an order, our attacks will be ready to launch within seconds.

AYAORI

In an emergency, America is also a type of dictatorship, so they will if they decide to.

KIM JONG-UN'S G.S.

Trump only has around 30 percent [approval rating], so he is already beaten. And the security costs to protect Trump Tower are so high that they are talking about withdrawing the police.

AYAORI

No, no. More than half of Americans are in favor of attacking North Korea. It came out in a public opinion poll.

KIM JONG-UN'S G.S.

No, I don't believe that. I mean, Texas is still flooded from that hurricane I sent.

AYAORI

Ah, you sent that? [*Laughs.*]

KIM JONG-UN'S G.S.

Of course I did.

AYAORI

How did you do that?

KIM JONG-UN'S G.S.

I am a god, so I can do anything. So, of course I can.

AYAORI

No [*laughs*], I don't believe you are that powerful.

KIM JONG-UN'S G.S.

The gods of Japan haven't been able to send typhoons to North Korea, right?

AYAORI

No, no. We're not sure yet. It's only just started.

KIM JONG-UN'S G.S.

My control extends all the way to the Mexican Gulf Stream, and it's easy to send hurricanes from there to attack Texas.

"Democracy values following due process. They must have a debate before retaliating"

YUKI OIKAWA

May I ask a question?

KIM JONG-UN'S G.S.

Yeah, sure.

OIKAWA

Chairman Kim, going back to something you said at the beginning, is it possible that North Korea might preemptively strike Yamaguchi Prefecture, Prime Minister Abe's hometown?

KIM JONG-UN'S G.S.

It's possible, it's possible. And if he retaliated because of it, he would be mixing his public and private life, from a Japanese point of view.

OIKAWA

I see. If...

KIM JONG-UN'S G.S.

As for me, I would not mix public and private matters. Public and private matters are a single thing to me. But if Abe became enraged and declared an all-out war just because his home was hit by a missile, that would be mixing public and private matters.

AYAORI

No, it wouldn't because it's Japanese territory [*laughs*].

KIM JONG-UN'S G.S.

No, that's not true. Even if it's inside the territory...

AYAORI

[*Laughs.*] He is responsible for Japan, so it doesn't matter where it is.

KIM JONG-UN'S G.S.

The only ones who would suffer would be Mr. Abe and his supporters.

OIKAWA

Chairman Kim, I would like to check your understanding once more. Don't you believe that, if a missile from North Korea were to hit Mr. Abe's hometown, or anywhere in the Japanese territory, America would immediately commence a counterattack in accordance with the right of collective self-defense? Have you not thought about this?

KIM JONG-UN'S G.S.

No, they can't do that if it only hits Abe's parents' home. They would suffer too much damage. The damage the American military would suffer would be too big.

OIKAWA

Earlier, you said that even if something like that happened, they would discuss it first at the UN...

KIM JONG-UN'S G.S.

That's right. I mean, the moment America starts showing signs as if they are about to attack, we will immediately attack Seoul and its surroundings. Not all of the Japanese people and Americans living in South Korea have escaped. There are still 50,000 to 60,000 Japanese people there, right? And I believe there are even more Americans. All of them would burn to death. Do you think they would allow that many Japanese and Americans to die just over Abe's neighborhood burning down?

We could kill them at ease. With my decision, they would be dead within ten minutes.

OIKAWA

So, in other words, you don't think America would retaliate, right?

KIM JONG-UN'S G.S.

No, because democracy values procedure. It is necessary to follow due process, and they would have to discuss whether or not to attack after passing it through Congress and the UN first and coming to a consensus.

AYAORI

America wouldn't go through that entire process one by one before starting a war.

KIM JONG-UN'S G.S.

They have to acquire a budget as well for the war. They'll need approval for their budget, their military budget.

OIKAWA

I see.

"Xi Jinping will overlook
A missile attack on Hong Kong"

OIKAWA

Incidentally, a government-affiliated newspaper in China recently reported that if North Korea were to conduct a preemptive strike and America retaliated, China would not interfere. If North Korea strikes first, America will probably retaliate immediately. In other words, what they are saying is that not even China can protect North Korea in that case.

KIM JONG-UN'S G.S.

However, China has never been an honest country, historically speaking. They usually say the opposite. They are just simply debating. But if that's the case, I might send Xi Jinping some support in the form of an "encouragement missile." Do you want to know how I think?

I said I would target Abe's home, and in the same vein, what I would do is launch a missile at Hong Kong. That would make Xi Jinping think, "Oh, he's shooting Hong Kong for me. That saves me a lot of trouble." See? By suffering this, Hong Kong would realize that they can't protect themselves if they don't stand together with Beijing. In other words, even if a missile were en route to attack Hong Kong, he would overlook it thinking, "Meh, it's just Hong Kong." Then it strikes and BOOM—tons of people's assets would be blown away. See? Then, Hong Kong would no longer function under "one country, two systems" but would instead settle as "one country, one system." Xi Jinping would enter his third term as president in comfort and ease.

OIKAWA

I see. It's an interesting idea.

KIM JONG-UN'S G.S.

Right? That's what I'm planning. That's why, no one will be able to stand against me unless he or she brings someone as resourceful as Yukimura Sanada.

"American aircraft carriers would be Like beehives"

OIKAWA

Chairman Kim, what if—as opposed to how you explained your understanding a moment ago—America is just waiting for North Korea to conduct a small preemptive strike before immediately unleashing a massive retaliation? If so, what would you do?

KIM JONG-UN'S G.S.

I would read the situation and plan my revenge. I already assume their likely action, so the next...

OIKAWA

What if America already sees that coming too?

KIM JONG-UN'S G.S.

Assuming that America will use an aircraft carrier to attack, we [North Korea] would send one of our submarines up next to it and hit it with a missile. BOOM! It would pierce right through the deck. This would be a sensational news to the world. They would be like, "Wow, one of America's aircraft carriers was sunk!" See? They want to fight using just two [aircraft carriers], right? Well, this would show them that we aren't the kind of country that they can attack using those.

OIKAWA

You seem to have quite a lot of confidence.

KIM JONG-UN'S G.S.

I think America's aircraft carriers will end up like beehives. Boom-boom-boom-boom. Eight or so missiles would come slamming down at a 90-degree angle, directly from above. They can't shoot the missiles down. Even if they did, it would still hit them.

South Korea's President Moon
Who calls for a talk is a "good prey"

OIKAWA

So, in other words, are you saying that you are competent enough to fight, should America and North Korea escalate into an all-out war?

KIM JONG-UN'S G.S.

Yes, we can win. First, we will weaken America's will to fight and have them run around in confusion. We will confuse Japan too, and just when everyone is on the phone having many conferences, we'll go and take South Korea in one fell swoop. Mark my words, we are going to take South Korea.

Once we have taken South Korea, it will be hard for the U.S. to attack because they won't be able to use their weapons of mass destruction against South Korea. We will flood into South Korea all at once. Then, it would be a similar situation again. Refugees will flee all the way to the southern portion of South Korea. Things will be surprisingly safe once we are in control of the country internally. I'd like to see if they can attack us. It'll just result in dead South Koreans. Go ahead. Hahaha [*laughs*].

KAZUHIRO ICHIKAWA

What do you think about President Moon?

KIM JONG-UN'S G.S.

Well, he's a really good prey. He's like a sheep that just wandered in. I feel like I can make as many threats as I want.

AYAORI

South Korea's President Moon is calling for a talk, even at this stage.

KIM JONG-UN'S G.S.

That guy is an idiot. He's just a moron.

AYAORI

[*Smiles wryly.*]

KIM JONG-UN'S G.S.

The South Korean citizens who elected him are even more stupid. So, yeah, from a leader like that, I could take the country. I will absolutely be able to take it easily.

AYAORI

I see.

KIM JONG-UN'S G.S.

Yeah, a single sheep like that is no match for a wolf. I can cook him up however I want.

What is North Korea's plan to annex South Korea in three days?

AYAORI

One of your ultimate goals is to annex South Korea, right?

KIM JONG-UN'S G.S.

Of course. I can't fight Japan and America unless I take South Korea. I will take South Korea. I will certainly take it.

AYAORI

I see.

KIM JONG-UN'S G.S.

I'll take it in about three days. Three days will be enough to take it.

AYAORI

So, once things escalate to an all-out war, you will head to South Korea, conquer it, prepare for a battle and then fight America and Japan?

KIM JONG-UN'S G.S.

I mean, I have a feeling America is waiting for the moment to assassinate me. But I have sixty body doubles. So, it's pretty hard to kill me. There will be people who look exactly like me appearing from here and there. So, it's not that easy.

Moon Jae-in hasn't even given a thought about how he might be assassinated. He needs to realize that I could take him down. It would be so easy to assassinate that idiot. If he were suddenly assassinated, the country would be unable to function. They wouldn't know what to do. There might also be anti-war demonstrations and so on. I have lots of spies like that in place, so anti-war demonstrations and movements like "Let's follow North Korea" and "Let's have them protect us" are...

AYAORI

According to your plan, how quickly do you hope to annex and secure South Korea?

KIM JONG-UN'S G.S.

I have studied the strategies of the Imperial Japanese Army, and I am well versed in it. The Imperial Japanese Army was adept at short and decisive battles that began from surprise attacks. I have done a lot of research into this, so we will do the kinds of things the Japanese army would. We might do something like the attack on Pearl Harbor.

AYAORI

Against America, right?

KIM JONG-UN'S G.S.

I don't know if it's America. The area around Seoul is currently on alert, but I wonder what they would do if we suddenly attacked Busan with a missile. I don't think they have considered it.

AYAORI

America would surely retaliate.

KIM JONG-UN'S G.S.

It'll take them time to do so.

AYAORI

That depends on President Trump. I believe that immediate retaliation followed by an all-out war is certainly within the realm of possibility.

KIM JONG-UN'S G.S.

I am fully confident that we can win.

AYAORI

Oh, I see.

KIM JONG-UN'S G.S.

We might simultaneously conduct another nuclear test at that time.

"We will nuke Busan and make Seoul surrender without bloodshed"

ICHIKAWA

Aside from missiles, you are currently conducting nuclear development behind the scenes, but how far have you gotten?

KIM JONG-UN'S G.S.

We are reaching the level of completion. So, we have to test it out. We never know unless we use it in an actual warfare once. We have to leave some of South Korea's prosperity intact. If we destroy it, there won't be any more games. We could drop a nuke in the south near Busan, but the majority of the people will be left unscathed. Just once I'd like to produce a mushroom cloud.

AYAORI

Are you saying you are going to nuke Busan?

KIM JONG-UN'S G.S.

Yeah. It wouldn't destroy all of South Korea. Then, what would happen is that Seoul would surrender without a fight.

AYAORI

I see.

KIM JONG-UN'S G.S.

My goal is to have Seoul give up without bloodshed, not Pyongyang. I want to "take it as a whole." I will also be the president.

AYAORI

Oh, really? But at that point, America might decide to...

KIM JONG-UN'S G.S.

No, the next hurricane might be coming.

AYAORI

I don't know about a hurricane, but there would be an all-out war and Pyongyang would get bombed. Various military bases would be bombed.

KIM JONG-UN'S G.S.

No, that won't happen. We have many bases aboveground and America believes that we have 150 missile sites, but we actually have many more. We have actually built many more, tunneling like moles. We have built a great number of underground passageways, too.

We are capable of resisting till the bitter end, so that we can use the same underground methods that successfully defeated America in the Vietnam War. We have also created many underground passageways that will let us escape to South Korea. So, North Korean ground forces will suddenly appear within South Korea and begin fighting. Our opponents won't know where to attack.

ICHIKAWA

You mentioned underground passageways, but according to one theory, you are rumored to have escape routes into China, and you will flee there if you have to.

KIM JONG-UN'S G.S.

I don't think I will need to flee. We are going to win, so I won't need to flee. Instead, actually, northeastern China... what's it called? The area that used to be called Manchuria. I am thinking about taking that area. That region doesn't necessarily obey Xi Jinping.

ICHIKAWA

You mean, the Shenyang Military Region?

KIM JONG-UN'S G.S.

Yeah. That area is somewhat independent since the people there are ethnically different to begin with. Also, there are many North Koreans who are there for work. A lot of people come and go for work, and a lot of undercover operatives as well. I think it might be a good idea to take that area in one go.

"North Korea is necessary for Putin and Xi Jinping Because they want to be in power for life"

OIKAWA

So, you say you have many more missile bases and underground facilities than America realizes.

KIM JONG-UN'S G.S.

That's right, yeah, yeah, yeah.

OIKAWA

But the current Trump administration plays things close to the chest. They release almost no information. They might already know everything. Aren't you afraid of that?

KIM JONG-UN'S G.S.

He keeps fighting with the press, and everyone is looking for a reason to impeach him, right? A war would be the biggest reason yet. Warmongering presidents create financial deficits.

AYAORI

Actually, I think it's the opposite. America comes together during times like that. You mentioned Pearl Harbor a moment ago. If you were to do something like that, you would be justifying America's attack. Japan already has experience with it, but the same thing would happen to North Korea.

KIM JONG-UN'S G.S.

But if an American aircraft carrier were to be sunk in the Sea of Japan, the footage of that would be shown all over the world. This would be pretty hard on them. They would find it difficult to continue fighting after that.

AYAORI

You know, you are very high-spirited every time...

KIM JONG-UN'S G.S.

Right now, Russia is being really cooperative. Russia.

AYAORI

True. Trade [between North Korea and Russia] has definitely increased.

KIM JONG-UN'S G.S.

They say it's Putin's fault that Trump is accused of Russiagate. Putin is angry about that. "It would be good for us to reconcile, but you're blaming it on me?" It's because he wants to be an emperor for life. Same with Xi Jinping. That's what he's aiming for, too. So, when you think about it, North Korea is necessary. No matter how you look at it.

"We have more than 10 times the mobility of and Are 100 times as decisive as a democratic nation"

OIKAWA

I certainly believe that Russia needs North Korea, but you seem excessively optimistic about all of this. Is that how you really feel? Are you truly that optimistic?

KIM JONG-UN'S G.S.

Well, at the very least, we have more than 10 times the mobility of and are 100 times as decisive as a democratic nation. I mean, we already have all the weapons we need. All we have to do is invent a way to monetize these weapons. It's a matter of how we need to fight in order for it to be lucrative. At the very least, we could take something as collateral and rake in money by asking for a ransom. Japan would fork over money immediately, right? If they are in trouble somehow...

OIKAWA

But the UN, which you mentioned earlier, agreed this month to apply economic sanctions against North Korea greater than any applied so far. Even China and Russia agreed. Doesn't that frighten you?

KIM JONG-UN'S G.S.

We will get around them, don't worry. North Korean hackers are currently considering ways of extracting electronic funds. We have amassed quite a budget, so don't think that the money that is inside North Korea is all the money we have. The members of our group stationed in other countries are quite talented, and they are particularly good at cyber-attacks and stealing intangible electronic funds. You need to realize that we still have access to that money.

"If we take South Korea and northeastern China, And launch attacks from there, There will be no counterattack"

OIKAWA

Nevertheless, the United Nations has said that it will impose financial sanctions on this occasion. Is that all right?

KIM JONG-UN'S G.S.

They don't really understand the true situation. INTERPOL [International Criminal Police Organization] is after some people, and the focus is on the crimes of individuals. They cannot track down crimes committed by a country. There are no organizational means or methods with regard to that.

It is done by a country. At the level of various countries, such as Bangladesh for example, things are managed very poorly, so it is easy to crack and steal from such countries. Thus, we can collect abundant funds and take them to other countries, and procure various items.

OIKAWA

I see. Aside from finances, the United Nations is attempting to prohibit almost all exporting and importing of goods with North Korea, and it appears that China will also participate in this. Is that all right?

KIM JONG-UN'S G.S.

That is how it looks on the surface. Behind the scenes we are able to receive supplies from pirate vessels, and we still have supplies from underground routes, so the official statistics show...

In your country, everyone is being monitored by the mass media and you may think it is harsh, but we don't have anything like "the mass media" in our country. We are not being monitored by anything like that. In China, the mass media do exactly what the top echelon wants them to do, so they can't act independently.

OIKAWA

China is currently under pressure from the Trump administration of the U.S. to do something about the trade deficit. Therefore, perhaps China will not be able to maintain its existing position regarding North Korea.

KIM JONG-UN'S G.S.

No, China has "military-first politics," so the economy does not come first. The military comes first. China understands that in spite of whatever Trump says, what he is aiming for next is the "dismantling of China."

Therefore, China might supply us via a "secret army."

OIKAWA

A secret army?

KIM JONG-UN'S G.S.

Yes. China might supply us via a "secret chivalrous army" or "chivalrous outlaws" that people don't know are from China.

OIKAWA

Will that alone be sufficient?

KIM JONG-UN'S G.S.

Yes, I think so. That is because we will take South Korea. We might at least take South Korea and northeastern China, and there is a possibility of our also receiving masked support from Russia. Therefore, we will just have to see how it goes.

I have enough confidence to start a fight.

ICHIKAWA

Are you thinking of an imperialistic hegemonic war after that?

KIM JONG-UN'S G.S.

First of all, South and North Koreas will be unified since we will take South Korea. Also, there are places in northeastern China that have become almost like North Korea, and if we can take them, we can get many weapons. There are military forces that don't obey what Xi Jinping says, and we might be able to get them to change sides. Since this is Chinese territory, if we launch an attack from there, the U.S. probably won't be able to act. This is what we have in mind.

"We also have the option of suddenly Firing missiles at China"

AYAORI

I think it is fine that you are very high-spirited and have a positive attitude, but it is being said that stealth bombers of the U.S. have recently flown in North Korean airspace many times, and have even flown above Pyongyang.

It is said that since you don't like that sound, you stated that you will strike Guam. But isn't it true that you can't sleep at night?

KIM JONG-UN'S G.S.

No, I think the person who can't sleep at night is Trump.

AYAORI

No, I don't think that's the case.

KIM JONG-UN'S G.S.

If his approval rating falls once more time, he will be in trouble. The mass media are aiming to get him fired, less than a year into his term. They are "fake news," right? All of the mass media in the U.S.

Our country does not have any problems like that. All people say, "We dedicate our life to comrade Kim Jong-un."

AYAORI

Yes, you're right.

KIM JONG-UN'S G.S.

We are similar to the Imperial Japanese Army. We are strong, strong, strong.

AYAORI

They were not that strong.

KIM JONG-UN'S G.S.

As Isoroku Yamamoto [an admiral of the Imperial Japanese Navy] said, we will fight for one or two years.

AYAORI

You won't last one or two years.

KIM JONG-UN'S G.S.

You don't know that. You don't know for sure. When we attack with our hydrogen bombs, I don't think the other countries will last for a year.

AYAORI

No, North Korea won't last.

KIM JONG-UN'S G.S.

Well, as a form of "ambush," we could "suddenly fire missiles at China." If we do that, China won't know which side to defend.

I know this because I have studied the Battle of Sekigahara*.

AYAORI

Really?

KIM JONG-UN'S G.S.

Yes. Tokugawa's Eastern Army was at a disadvantage, so they got the enemy to change sides. They fired cannons, right? Hideaki Kobayakawa of the Western Army changed sides.

Therefore, we also have the option of firing at China if China is indecisive. China may suddenly shape up and return to their senses.

---

* Most decisive battle of the Sengoku period in Japan, in the year 1600, that took place in Sekigahara [Gifu Prefecture]. Many Daimyo split and fought on either the Western or the Eastern Army. The Eastern Army led by Ieyasu Tokugawa achieved victory, giving rise to Tokugawa Shogunate.

Collaboration with countries that are upset about The high-handedness of the U.S.

AYAORI

Meanwhile, China is also thinking about removing you.

KIM JONG-UN'S G.S.

That would not be good, so to avoid that, I got rid of my older brother Kim Jong-nam.

AYAORI

You acted preemptively.

KIM JONG-UN'S G.S.

I know that all my relatives are thinking of installing a puppet to take my place. China and the U.S. are also thinking that. That is why I have eliminated most of the people who could potentially be installed as a puppet.

AYAORI

There are still other candidates, so assassinating you and installing another leader under China's initiative is being considered...

KIM JONG-UN'S G.S.

If I am removed, it will be a situation like in Iraq. There will be hand-to-hand combat everywhere like with ISIS or IS, and several million people will die. Americans will also die one after another, and it will be like the Vietnam War. You want to avoid that, right?

AYAORI

Even inside North Korea, there are groups who are fed up with you and want to remove you.

KIM JONG-UN'S G.S.

No. As soon as those people are found, they are executed on the same day, right away.

AYAORI

I don't think it is that easy.

KIM JONG-UN'S G.S.

We have already executed many of those people.

AYAORI

I see.

KIM JONG-UN'S G.S.

Yes.

AYAORI

Nonetheless, there are many of those people. Groups of elders and so on from a long time ago would like to remove you.

KIM JONG-UN'S G.S.

First of all, there are still a few foreign guests here. There are many foreign guests in the area around Pyongyang, so I think we should offer them some "hospitality."

AYAORI

I believe that, in fact, there are many people around you— including in China—who think that the current regime should come to an end.

KIM JONG-UN'S G.S.

That is not the case. Russia wants to use us as a shield, and Iran actually wants to connect with us. Iran and Egypt are actually upset about the high-handed methods of the U.S.

AYAORI

That may be true of countries that buy weapons from North Korea.

KIM JONG-UN'S G.S.

They are very upset about the sense of discrimination against the Islamic world. If we connect with all of them and integrate with Iran's Islamic terrorism, amazing things could happen. There could be a simultaneous revolution worldwide.

Japan is a minor power in the world That only tries to make money

OIKAWA

Before that, China seems to already be thinking about what will come after your regime. They might be thinking that, rather than the Kim family, an ordinary military regime would be acceptable. Therefore, China is probably thinking about using someone to create a military regime, and anyone would be acceptable as long as that person is under Chinese control.

KIM JONG-UN'S G.S.

If that is the case, it will probably lead to a conflict between China and the U.S.

OIKAWA

What if the U.S. were to permit China to do that?

KIM JONG-UN'S G.S.

That would be dangerous for them. This is because China is more dangerous than North Korea. If all North Korean nuclear missiles were entrusted to China, then South Korea and Japan would probably be in mortal fear.

OIKAWA

What if the U.S. and China agreed to stop your country's nuclear development from progressing any further?

KIM JONG-UN'S G.S.

They can't stop us because it is already an accomplished fact that we are a major nuclear power in the world. We are already recognized as a major military power, even by the countries of Europe. That's because it's known that we have nuclear weapons.

We should be accepted as a permanent member of the UN Security Council. Japan has lost their rights. It is a minor power that has to be defended by other countries. Due to its sin of only trying to make money, it will soon receive divine punishment.

We are basically already on track to becoming a permanent member of the UN Security Council. Therefore, it is only natural that South Korea will be unified with us, in light of our power.

OIKAWA

I think that is exactly what the international community wants to avoid the most.

KIM JONG-UN'S G.S.

The international community is wrong. It's a matter of self-government. For South Korea, the unification of the Korean Peninsula by North Korea is an ethnic wish. Putin understands this, and Xi Jinping also understands this because he has been doing many things along these lines up to now. It's natural.

The president of South Korea still has family in North Korea and strongly wants to be unified, so I feel that we must fulfill his wish.

The slow Japanese government that will introduce Aegis Ashore in five years

OIKAWA

The Trump administration of the U.S. has been saying that if you simply abandon your nuclear weapons program, it would be open to holding negotiations. What do you think about that?

KIM JONG-UN'S G.S.

That is of course a lie. That is foolish. If they think I have such low intelligence that they can fool me with tricks and words, they are seriously mistaken.

Trump is the type of person who gambles—sometimes wins and sometimes loses, just like playing cards. I am more precise. I carefully plan strategies and carry them out.

OIKAWA

Meanwhile, the Trump administration has been thinking about using military force if you don't hold talks. Aren't you afraid of that?

KIM JONG-UN'S G.S.

At this point, there won't be any talks. We are continuing to win. The fact is just accumulating, that's all. Look at Japan. They have been talking about Aegis Ashore, a land-based system with an Aegis function that shoots down missiles which Aegis ships alone can't shoot down. They are saying that they will introduce that in five years. The Japanese cabinet and government are too slow to be our enemy. Shall we kill all of them for you? We feel sorry for your tragic situation.

If Japan equips nuclear weapons, We will encourage anti-nuclear movements in Japan by firing missiles

AYAORI

If Japan were to take some type of action, what would bother you the most?

KIM JONG-UN'S G.S.

What would bother me the most would be if *Sankei Shimbun*[*] were to be destroyed by a fire. That would be bad. If Sankei Shimbun were to burn down, that would be the worst. I would be sad because there would no longer be people who criticize me. I would feel lonely. An office building like theirs could be destroyed with a single shot.

AYAORI

What if, for example, Japan declared to equip nuclear weapons?

KIM JONG-UN'S G.S.

How many years would that take?

AYAORI

I mean if Japan were to declare that.

---

* A newspaper publisher that Ayaori used to work for. Here, Kim Jong-un is playing with Ayaori.

KIM JONG-UN'S G.S.

After declaring that, how many years would that take?

AYAORI

It would be possible in 6 months to a year at the earliest.

KIM JONG-UN'S G.S.

Japan can make a declaration, but after the declaration, it could take 2 years, or maybe 5 or 10 years to make nuclear weapons. It isn't clear. It is wishful thinking for you to think that your country will still exist at that point. We already have nuclear weapons. We have them.

AYAORI

But with the power of the Japan Self-Defense Forces [JSDF], we can defeat North Korea.

KIM JONG-UN'S G.S.

Japan isn't even in the stage to develop nuclear weapons; there have been opposition movements with regard to the current nuclear power plants. Just firing a cheap missile someplace close to such places would trigger anti-nuclear movements all over Japan. That is what we are considering as the next effective strategy.

AYAORI

I see. OK.

KIM JONG-UN'S G.S.

Yes. Just firing a missile nearby would be enough. It doesn't have to hit, just dropping it nearby would be enough.

Japan, the world's weakest nation that has Inherited the worst aspects of the West

ICHIKAWA

Nevertheless, a portion of the people in Japan say, "Japan has a pacifist constitution, so a war cannot occur. There will be peace."

KIM JONG-UN'S G.S.

Ha-ha! [*Laughs.*] Stupid citizens like that should all be killed. What is it with them? It is as if they are saying, "We don't need a fence," even though the wolves have arrived. The stable doesn't need a fence.

AYAORI

What do you think of the revision to Article 9 of the Japanese Constitution that Prime Minister Abe is proposing?

KIM JONG-UN'S G.S.

It is too late.

AYAORI

He is proposing to add a third paragraph to make a clear statement regarding JSDF...

KIM JONG-UN'S G.S.

That is irrelevant. It seems very late to be placing the self-defense forces, which already exist, into the constitution. Such way of thinking is 50 years behind.

We are quicker. Perhaps you should declare a military-first government.

AYAORI

"The right of belligerency of the state will not be recognized" and "war potential will never be maintained" will remain in the constitution.

KIM JONG-UN'S G.S.

You are all truly brainwashed. You have inherited the worst aspects of the West. You currently have the slowest, weakest system. Japan is truly the weakest in the world.

AYAORI

I agree with you on that point.

KIM JONG-UN'S G.S.

You are the weakest in the world. You are the weakest nation. All you have is money. It is as if you want to have it taken. You have introduced electronic money and Bitcoin and are doing various things. We will be able to steal all of that from now on.

AYAORI

I see. That is what you are aiming for.

KIM JONG-UN'S G.S.

Really, the day will come when the Japanese economy is destroyed.

AYAORI

I see.

OIKAWA

In that sense, the recent North Korean crisis has greatly contributed to the revision of Article 9 of the Japanese Constitution...

KIM JONG-UN'S G.S.

Article 9 of the constitution doesn't matter anymore. It doesn't matter at all to me whether it exists or not. You don't understand that what you are even talking about is too late.

OIKAWA

Yes, it is late.

KIM JONG-UN'S G.S.

Yes, it is too late, so it is unnecessary. You should abolish the constitution. If it were me, I would abolish it in a single day. I am very quick. If I say we don't need it, then it is the end of story. You can't do that. You have been doing this for decades. Do you intend to do this for another hundred years?

It can't be helped. You have no choice but to perish. A race like that should perish. They are not needed.

Calling upon Japan to surrender and fall Under the control of North Korea

OIKAWA

Going back to what we talked about in the beginning, are you afraid of a preemptive attack by the U.S.?

KIM JONG-UN'S G.S.

Well, unless they attack first, there's no way they can win.

AYAORI

I see.

KIM JONG-UN'S G.S.

Yes. If North Korea carries out a preemptive attack, there is no way the U.S. can win. The allies of the U.S. will already be in ruins due to our preemptive attack, so defense will not be possible, and there will be nothing left to defend. There will only be a battle with the main part of the U.S., the mainland. Even if they win in the end, the U.S. would have lost their hegemony in the world. There would be no countries that believe in the U.S.

OIKAWA

That seems to mean there is a possibility the U.S. will carry out a preemptive attack.

KIM JONG-UN'S G.S.

I don't know about that. I could have my body doubles "executed" and throw the U.S. off guard, while I actually give commands from 150 meters underground.

OIKAWA

Do you have any plans to go out in public?

KIM JONG-UN'S G.S.

Officially, it is always said that I am present whenever a missile is launched, but you don't know if that is really me.

OIKAWA

No, we don't know.

KIM JONG-UN'S G.S.

You don't know. I could be replaced by someone in the photos that are released.

OIKAWA

But you can't continue that forever, can you?

KIM JONG-UN'S G.S.

Well, it's fun. It is like I am using a "multi-clone technique" where you can't tell if it's me, so it is fun. That's why you can't do anything to me. Hurry up and surrender. Japan's surrender would be the best for world peace. Japan should surrender and fall under the control of North Korea. Promise us that you will continue to provide us with trillions of yen in economic aid each year. Based on this, once Prime Minister Abe receives my words that Japan will not be the target of a nuclear attack or missiles, he can continue as prime minister.

OIKAWA

I see. This is directed to the current Japan, right?

KIM JONG-UN'S G.S.

Yes, it is.

A Trump assassination unit has been sent To the U.S.

OIKAWA

What do you want to say to the Trump administration?

KIM JONG-UN'S G.S.

Eventually, Trump will resign. Considering his physique, I think he will die from a heart attack soon. If a war were to start, he would probably die right away. In Trump Tower, he would probably be dead like a bug. And we have sent an assassination unit to the U.S.

AYAORI

You said that the last time as well [as already cited, see "North Korea in Crisis: A Spiritual Interview with the Guardian Spirit of Kim Jong-un"].

KIM JONG-UN'S G.S.

Yes. We have many people of various nationalities, so the person who kills him will not necessarily be North Korean. We can even have a Mexican kill him. There are many, many

Mexican hit men, and all we need to do is to give money. If I say, "I'll give you a million dollars," they will try to assassinate Trump.

The U.S. will probably become an enemy of Mexico. They are busy with work, saying, "The wall needs to be built faster."

OIKAWA

Before President Trump is assassinated, what if the U.S. were to carry out a preemptive attack greater than what you are envisioning?

KIM JONG-UN'S G.S.

Well, when I do appear in public, I am very careful, and it is difficult to confirm whether it is really me. When I appear in public, even Trump says, "The shape of his ears seems different somehow. I don't know if that's really him." They have trouble identifying me because they can't confirm that. That's right. There are various types. Some have undergone plastic surgery.

We are taking sufficient caution, so that we are not defeated with one shot in a preemptive attack. I will never be clumsy like Saddam Hussein. In the worst-case scenario, I can escape to China, South Korea, or Russia.

OIKAWA

I see.

If the Kanto region is struck with a nuclear weapon 1,000 times the power of the bombs on Hiroshima And Nagasaki, it will be completely destroyed

OIKAWA

This year in Afghanistan, a new bomb of the U.S. called "MOAB [Massive Ordnance Air Blast]" was used. It is apparently called the "Mother of All Bombs." What will you do if that is used on you?

KIM JONG-UN'S G.S.

That is cowardly. They only want to assert that it is not a nuclear weapon, right? We don't hesitate to use nuclear weapons. We will use both atomic bombs and hydrogen bombs.

It will not be like Hiroshima or Nagasaki. We currently have bombs with 1,000 times the power of those bombs. You should worry about the Kanto region being completely destroyed. After we completely destroy the Kanto region, even if you succeed in killing me in a war, it will already be game over for Japan.

OIKAWA

Do you have a plan to have someone carry out the attack later on, even if you are killed?

KIM JONG-UN'S G.S.

We will do it before I am killed. I am not that stupid. You should be aware that Japan's Kanto region will be gone before I am assassinated. That's why you have no choice but to surrender right now. You should believe that I, Chairman Kim, am the true savior of the world, and surrender.

North Korean strategy referring to the fighting style Of the Imperial Japanese Army

AYAORI

I think some of the things you said today actually have a possibility of succeeding.

KIM JONG-UN'S G.S.

What I said is logical, isn't it? You can tell that I have an IQ over 200 as you hear me. It's just that I don't want to see Sankei Shimbun destroyed by fire.

AYAORI

Nonetheless, it is clear that you hardly have any type of plans that will succeed over the long term.

KIM JONG-UN'S G.S.

Well, it will be a short-term, concentrated attack.

AYAORI

A concentrated attack?

KIM JONG-UN'S G.S.

That is a traditional way of fighting that I learned from the Armed Forces of the Empire of Japan.

AYAORI

We can say that if the U.S. were to seriously use all of their power, that strategy would fall apart in an instant.

KIM JONG-UN'S G.S.

You don't know that.

AYAORI

You mentioned earlier that you have made preparations to escape, and I think that is exactly what could happen.

KIM JONG-UN'S G.S.

Trump is the one who will try to escape, and he probably won't be able to escape to New York or Florida. He has to think about where he will try to go. We can even attack Alaska.

AYAORI

That would be the case if a full-scale war breaks out. But I think that if the U.S. takes serious action and Japan behaves more properly, there won't be any problem.

KIM JONG-UN'S G.S.

I am strong, so I could play the "strike Trump's bases in New York and Florida" card. I'm sure he'll be surprised.

AYAORI

Is that how you will threaten him?

KIM JONG-UN'S G.S.

New York's police force would be overwhelmed by our missiles.

AYAORI

Such threats might be effective.

KIM JONG-UN'S G.S.

It would be very difficult to defend against that. They would have to patrol the air above.

AYAORI

Later on, the guardian spirit of President Trump will be summoned. I don't think you should underestimate him. The same goes for Japan.

KIM JONG-UN'S G.S.

You should be aware that currently, North Korea is fighting on equal terms with or at a level above the U.S. You are just... We are stirring up fear because of you. We know that regardless of how many strong statements Prime Minister Abe makes, he can't do anything.

AYAORI

You are currently working hard to stir up fear. We take it that you stirred up a lot of fear today.

KIM JONG-UN'S G.S.

If you are afraid, load a lot of money onto Ospreys and drop it on us from the sky, instead of bombs.

AYAORI

Money? [*Smiles wryly.*]

KIM JONG-UN'S G.S.

Put cash on parachutes and drop it onto Pyongyang.

AYAORI

We won't do anything meaningless like that.

Challenging Japanese Shinto's Goddess Amaterasu to a spiritual battle

AYAORI

I would like for you to tell me. Who are you speaking with currently, regarding your various strategies and your future plans?

KIM JONG-UN'S G.S.

What do you mean by "who"?

AYAORI

You are the guardian spirit of Chairman Kim Jong-un. Who do you regularly speak to [in the Spirit World]?

KIM JONG-UN'S G.S.

Well, the first leader who was called the "Father of the nation," as well as the second and the third leaders, have all come together to speak about protecting the country.

AYAORI

Ah, OK. Kim Il-sung and Kim Jong-il, right?

KIM JONG-UN'S G.S

Currently, we are provoking the Japanese Shinto Goddess Amaterasu.* "If you are frustrated, then make Mt. Baekdu

---

* The Sun Goddess who is the principal goddess of Japanese Shinto.

erupt. I will make Mt. Fuji erupt. Let's have a spiritual battle to see who is stronger."

AYAORI

Oh, it's a spiritual battle?

KIM JONG-UN'S G.S.

It's to see which god is the true god. Yeah.

AYAORI

OK.

KIM JONG-UN'S G.S.

Making Mt. Fuji erupt is one of the options, if we are stronger. Hmph!

AYAORI

I don't think you can do it.

KIM JONG-UN'S G.S.

It must be frightening. The eruption of Mt. Fuji is even scarier than a nuke.

Dragging the U.S. into hand-to-hand combat, Similar to the Vietnam War

AYAORI

I take it that you have come to make various threats today.

KIM JONG-UN'S G.S.

You should analyze my thinking pattern. You will see that I have thoughts that do not exist within your brains. You will understand that I am a genius.

OIKAWA

At the same time, I can see that you are very optimistic.

KIM JONG-UN'S G.S.

Well, since America... Well, America must be tamed. It is an era when they must be disciplined.

AYAORI

At the same time, I believe that you are slightly desperate.

KIM JONG-UN'S G.S.

Well, that's not true. I am not like that. Even Vietnam was able to win. I believe that we can win against America. Yeah.

ICHIKAWA

With this much confidence, you must have something grand, like a secret agreement, with China backing you up as your rear shield.

KIM JONG-UN'S G.S.

I believe that we can fight well just by ourselves. Even in Vietnam, they didn't have much in terms of weaponry, right? It was pretty much a battle fought within a few hundred kilometers of underground passages. Plus, if you ask whether we have underground passages, we do. We are also able to escape to South Korea, so there are places to escape everywhere.

What America fears the most is to be drawn into hand-to-hand combat on the Korean Peninsula. If it develops into hand-to-hand combat, the battle will not end even if they send 30,000 or 50,000 troops. They wouldn't be able to make a nuclear attack while their troops are battling. This is what they really fear. If a 10-year-long hand-to-hand combat were to start, the U.S. would have to deploy millions, who would die. This is something they would rather avoid. This is why we are thinking of that option. Yeah.

It will take Japan at least 10 years to Prepare the legal system

AYAORI

I believe that we have been taught about what America dislikes, and what are effective as threats today.

KIM JONG-UN'S G.S.

We fire missiles, but at times, they go off track, or off the flight path. They veer off the calculations slightly. One in every few launches goes off track.

AYAORI

Well, their accuracy is not great.

KIM JONG-UN'S G.S.

I believe that we should "avoid hitting the premises of Sankei Shimbun." This is the only company that claims the right thing, isn't it? It's a newspaper company, right? If we hit it, there will no longer be any place that will criticize North Korea. There is a chance that even though we were trying to hit *Asahi Shimbun* [a newspaper company], we accidently hit Sankei Shimbun. Hmm...

AYAORI

I don't think it would affect that many people [*laughs*].

KIM JONG-UN'S G.S.

There is a possibility that missiles will conveniently be guided toward people who are badmouthing us. This is fine, right?

AYAORI

In a sense, I understand what kind of state of mind you're in.

KIM JONG-UN'S G.S.

Do not treat a 34-year-old the same as a 71-year-old geezer. I can still fight for 35 years.

AYAORI

On the contrary, I can also imagine that you are being cornered.

KIM JONG-UN'S G.S.

Nope, I am calm and composed. So, watch me as I sink aircraft carriers. I will sink American aircraft carriers, about two of them. With this, the world will tremble. I will teach everyone that the era of aircraft carriers has ended.

AYAORI

I understand now that you have this aim as well.

KIM JONG-UN'S G.S.

Next, I will experiment on firing missiles from submarines. Hehehe [*laughs*].

AYAORI

I see. Now I understand that you will have various tasks you will start up.

KIM JONG-UN'S G.S.

Yeah, yeah. I will not lose. I will attack in short, concentrated attacks when striking first, but when drawn into a long-term ground battle, the U.S. is the one who will suffer.

AYAORI

Yes, there are possibilities of this.

KIM JONG-UN'S G.S.

The Americans don't want to die anymore. They don't want to die.

AYAORI

Yes, this may be true, but the U.S. would also have thought up measures against this.

KIM JONG-UN'S G.S.

It will take at least 10 years for Japan to prepare the legal system. This is not even worth talking about.

AYAORI

Yes, I will honestly accept this point. We are thinking about what we can do.

KIM JONG-UN'S G.S.

You must understand that you are the weakest in the world. Japan only has money, and is the weakest country in the world. You must understand this.

AYAORI

I would like to humbly accept these words. OK, thank you.

KIM JONG-UN'S G.S.

So, are we done?

Kim Jong-un, who is in his first half of his thirties, Is not afraid of anything

RYUHO OKAWA

[*Claps three times.*] Well, he has a lot of vigor. He must be eating good food. He is probably eating very good food.

Certainly, the first half of your thirties is a period of time when you are physically and intellectually very motivated, so he is not afraid of anything. Next, let us speak with the guardian spirit of President Trump. I think he would prefer English.

Chapter Two

Spiritual Interview with the Guardian Spirit of Donald Trump

The contents of hard-line measures that remind us of the Cuban Missile Crisis

Recorded August 29, 2017
Happy Science General Headquarters,
Japan

Donald Trump (1946-Present)

American politician and businessman. Belongs to the Republican Party. The 45th president of the United States of America. Born in New York. After graduating from the University of Pennsylvania in 1968, Trump entered his father's real estate company and was given a controlling interest in 1971. Starting with the completion of "the world's most luxurious building" Trump Tower on the Fifth Avenue of New York in 1983, he experienced major success with real estate related business and hotel and casino management, generating millions of dollars in wealth and earning the name "Real Estate King." On January 20, 2017, he was inaugurated as the 45th president of the United States of America.

Interviewers from Happy Science*:

Yuki Oikawa
Director of Foreign Affairs
Happiness Realization Party

Kazuhiro Ichikawa
Senior Managing Director
Chief Director of International Headquarters

Jiro Ayaori
Managing Director
Chief Editor of *The Liberty*
Lecturer of Happy Science University

The opinions of the spirit do not necessarily reflect those of Happy Science Group.

---

* The interviewer's professional title represents the position at the time of the interview.

We can destroy them within three days

RYUHO OKAWA

Then, I will summon the guardian spirit of Mr. Donald Trump.

The guardian spirit of Mr. Donald Trump,

Would you come down here?

We are Happy Science.

We want to know what you are thinking in your mind. Could you please teach us what you are thinking about now?

TRUMP'S GUARDIAN SPIRIT

Hmm.

YUKI OIKAWA

Mr. President?

TRUMP'S G.S.

Hmm. Hmm.

OIKAWA

First of all, Hurricane Harvey.

TRUMP'S G.S.

Hi. Hurricane?

OIKAWA

I think your leadership of the rescue activities and the people's power are amazing.

TRUMP'S G.S.

Amazing... Amazing! Good.

OIKAWA

So, during your very busy time, we would like to ask you about the very important issue of North Korea. Is that OK?

TRUMP'S G.S.

OK. No problem.

OIKAWA

All right. So, we just talked with the guardian spirit of Kim Jong-un. Did you hear our conversation?

TRUMP'S G.S.

A little.

OIKAWA

OK. So, what is your comment?

TRUMP'S G.S.

Hahaha [*laughs*]. Ah, he is very weak. A weak dog barks well. That's all.

OIKAWA

Why do you think he's weak?

TRUMP'S G.S.

Because he talks too much. We'll never be frightened by his threats, by their old-fashioned nuclear weapon.

OIKAWA

I see. He was trying to hide his real intention. Maybe he has some kind of fear toward you.

TRUMP'S G.S.

If we decide to conduct justice of the world, we can destroy them within three days.

OIKAWA

Three days?

TRUMP'S G.S.

Three days.

OIKAWA

OK. OK. So, let me ask about the nuclear development in North Korea. Do you expect North Korea to give up their nuclear development?

TRUMP'S G.S.

They are liars. We cannot believe them.

OIKAWA

So, you don't believe they will give up nuclear weapons in the future?

TRUMP'S G.S.

Already his ancestor, the first Kim... Kim... I don't know. His grandfather...

OIKAWA

Kim Il-sung?

TRUMP'S G.S.

Oh, Kim Il-sung. He made agreement regarding the abolishment of nuclear power*, but he lied. [*Clicks tongue.*] So, the same.

We will destroy all of North Korea with ICBMs By the end of 2017

OIKAWA

OK. Formally, your government, the U.S. government, is

---

* Kim Il-sung had announced at U.S.-North Korea talks that he was ready to freeze the nuclear development program. However, he suddenly passed in 1994 and Kim Jong-il formally signed the agreement.

having negotiations with North Korea in order to force them to give up nuclear weapons, but you already realized they will never give up. I see. OK. In that case, what is your strategy?

TRUMP'S G.S.
We will use ICBMs first.

OIKAWA
Right.

TRUMP'S G.S.
We don't use PAC-3. We use ICBMs. From the west side of the United States, we will dispatch maybe 10 or 20 ICBMs and destroy all the important facilities of North Korea.

OIKAWA
OK. Are you talking about your preemptive attack?

TRUMP'S G.S.
It's a top secret, so it's very difficult.

OIKAWA
I know, but...

TRUMP'S G.S.

I want to be honest because Mr. Ryuho Okawa of Happy Science did a good lecture regarding me. Mr. Okawa said Donald Trump is an honest man, so I want to be honest, but this is top secret. But I, myself, have decided in me, the death of Kim Jong-un will come soon.

OIKAWA

How soon?

TRUMP'S G.S.

[*Laughs.*] It's top-secret. If I say something, he can make a preemptive attack.

OIKAWA

Within this year?

TRUMP'S G.S.

Of course.

OIKAWA

Of course?

TRUMP'S G.S.

Of course.

KAZUHIRO ICHIKAWA

How will you end the Kim regime of North Korea?

TRUMP'S G.S.

Oh, it will see the ruins of the Kim Jong-un regime. Only the ruins can be seen on earth from the satellite. You cannot find his dead body because there can be only ruins, the ruins of the losers. The old city which was called Pyongyang.

One million people of North Korea will die

JIRO AYAORI

So, if the Korean War restarted, it is said that almost one million people would be dead.

TRUMP'S G.S.

Ah, one million people of North Korea.

AYAORI

Oh.

OIKAWA

Not South Korea?

TRUMP'S G.S.

North Korea.

OIKAWA

Why? Why do you think you can rescue the people in Seoul? Even if you start...

TRUMP'S G.S.

I'm not Obama, you know? Obama just attacked Osama bin Laden, but I will do our best. When I take action, it means the death of North Korea.

OIKAWA

People think that when the U.S. starts the preemptive attack on North Korea, many people will die because of the revenge attack on South Korea and Japan.

TRUMP'S G.S.

No, no, no, no. There is no North Korea in the near future, so you are safe.

OIKAWA

Because the war with...

We will destroy all the country.
North Korea will disappear from the world map

TRUMP'S G.S.

I mean, I will destroy them completely. The country, the leaders, and of course, the people who supported them.

OIKAWA

I see. By your ICBMs?

TRUMP'S G.S.

Hmm.

OIKAWA

So, you don't have to use any other weapons of mass destruction?

TRUMP'S G.S.

I don't think there is another way, for example, to protect Guam like that, or to protect Japan. No. I'll attack and destroy North Korea.

OIKAWA

I see.

TRUMP'S G.S.

That is my decision. I'm the leader of the world. My decision is the decision of God!

OIKAWA

I see. Right. Coming back to our conversation with Kim Jong-un's guardian spirit, he said, "Maybe the United States thinks there are more than 150 military bases in North Korea, but we have more."

TRUMP'S G.S.

Hmm.

OIKAWA

So, what do you think about that? You know more...

TRUMP'S G.S.

OK, no problem. We will destroy all the country.

OIKAWA

All over the country?

TRUMP'S G.S.

Oh, yeah. The country of North Korea will disappear from the world map.

OIKAWA

I see. That is your strategy?

TRUMP'S G.S.

Hmm.

OIKAWA

OK. So, in that case, we have to realize it will include innocent people.

TRUMP'S G.S.

It's OK, no problem. They were guilty when they were born in North Korea.

OIKAWA

Are you afraid...

TRUMP'S G.S.

It's destiny for them. Bye-bye [*waves his hand*].

OIKAWA

I see, I see. Do you feel any concern for the people in Seoul? They are families of the U.S. military.

TRUMP'S G.S.

It's OK. Our attack is great-power ICBMs and they will

completely destroy all the nation of North Korea, so the people who live in Seoul or Japan are perfectly safe.

OIKAWA

Perfectly?

TRUMP'S G.S.

I guarantee. He thinks too small, technical war. He is just thinking, "Just attack our military forces, islands, vessels, bombing aircraft or things like that." But our attack shall completely destroy them. That is the final answer from me.

If the U.S. makes a small attack, China will think little of our force

AYAORI

In such a case, is it possible to fight against the Chinese military? What do you think about that situation?

TRUMP'S G.S.

Next. It will come next. But when we sweep them away easily, China will become calm and very easy to be handled with. I think so.

ICHIKAWA

So, in order to attack North Korea, what do you expect of Japan and South Korea?

TRUMP'S G.S.

No, I will not explain anything because they speak a lot. So, it's a secret. After that, we will lecture them, "That is the reason why Pyongyang disappeared from this world." I will explain after that.

OIKAWA

OK. So, we should understand that your strategy is, maybe all of a sudden, you will begin an attack? Am I right?

TRUMP'S G.S.

All of a sudden? No. People of the world already know about that. More than 50% think I will attack them. All the people of the world understand.

OIKAWA

Yeah, they already understand.

TRUMP'S G.S.

Yeah, yeah. So, Kim Jong-un is just checking my braveness. He wants to play chicken, but this is not a chicken game. It's their death ONLY!

OIKAWA

I see. So, anytime from now until the end of this year, we could see the death of Kim Jong-un? Is that right?

TRUMP'S G.S.

No. Almost all of North Korean people. That's the strategy.

OIKAWA

OK. So, by doing that strategy, or after you succeed in your strategy, what will happen to North Korea?

TRUMP'S G.S.

There is no North Korea.

OIKAWA

No people?

TRUMP'S G.S.

No people.

OIKAWA

So, how are you gonna...

TRUMP'S G.S.

South Korea will govern North Korea, or the North Korean people who were left and survived our nuclear attack.

OIKAWA

So, in that case, the U.S. forces will stay in the Korean Peninsula? I mean, China is really afraid of... you know, after the war, after your victory, the U.S. military will come very close to the border between China and North Korea. That's what they're afraid of. So...

TRUMP'S G.S.

If we make a small attack on them, China would think little of our force, but if we use nuclear attack, they will keep silence. I think so.

OIKAWA

Silence?

TRUMP'S G.S.

Next Hiroshima and Nagasaki will appear in North Korea, so we will govern them.

OIKAWA

Govern the peninsula?

TRUMP'S G.S.

We will make the peninsula of Korea like the Japanese... They will again make a recovery from ruins, and like Japan, they can redevelop. So, that is my strategy. It's simple.

My main point is to end Chinese totalitarianism

OIKAWA

I see. I see. So, you mean, if your strategy succeeds, China will be under big threat from you, and then China will allow you to govern the whole peninsula with South Korea. Is that right?

TRUMP'S G.S.

[*Sighs.*] OK. Xi Jinping is one of my friends. When he relies on and hears my words correctly, he is my good friend. If he disregards my saying, it is the beginning of his collapse, I mean, he will lose his political power in the near future.

America, the United States is quite different. I am not Obama. Obama will lose, but I'll never lose. I can save Japan. I can save South Korea. If some people survive after our attack, I will save such kind of North Korean people.

Of course, I'll change China's strategy for the future. They will make their gear change into the Western type of democracy. This is my main point. The attack on North Korea will change them. I think so. They are totalitarianism. China, also, is like that, so totalitarianism of the Chinese also must be changed from Xi Jinping regime to Hong Kong-like regime.

OIKAWA

Don't you think that, after the Kim Jong-un regime, China will intervene in building a new nation in the Korean Peninsula?

TRUMP'S G.S.

No, no, no. No possibility. They cannot win against our strategic military force. We have thousands of missiles or ICBMs, but they have only 400... It's just defensive ones, defensive missiles. But we have thousands of missiles. We can destroy all over China. It's impossible.

The Chinese economy is on the palm of my own

ICHIKAWA

About the future of North Korea, do you have any agreement under the table with China?

TRUMP'S G.S.
No.

ICHIKAWA

How about Russia? Did you talk to Mr. Putin about North Korea?

TRUMP'S G.S.

Russia is a very small... smaller country in the economic meaning and they only just show their political power using military power, but the end of the military power of Russia is coming soon. The starting point is the ruins of North Korea. I will destroy the military powers of China and Russia, also. Both of them.

The world should be led by us, the United States. We are the country of God and we have great reliance between Japan and the U.S., so we will make a new age as Mr. Ryuho Okawa said already, we will lead the next 300 years with our freedom and democratic system, and of course the liberalism within. We can make the world wealthier and make the happiness greater.

OIKAWA

On the other hand, you have another big issue. You have a huge trade deficit with China, so you have to deal with this issue as well.

TRUMP'S G.S.

It's OK, no problem. It's OK. At any time, we can make the deficit smaller than now because if we can be the top leader of the world, we can change the system, of course. For example, the foreign exchange rate, how to use the tariff system, or how to make the United Nations or other organizations. It depends on me. So, I can handle easily the Chinese economy. They are on the palm of my own.

OIKAWA

So, China will have to face huge pressure from your administration, right?

TRUMP'S G.S.

Yeah. That is the reason I appeared as a president of the U.S.

The U.S. and Japan can make a new world

AYAORI

What is your strategy to end the totalitarian state of China?

TRUMP'S G.S.

Firstly, the miserable result of North Korea will lead them to change their future. I think so. That kind of "military first" system is old-fashioned. It's the end of the Mao Zedong thinking. So, China should change and they should believe in God. That is my aim and my main point.

China needs a new God or religion, an orthodox religion. I think so. They need religion. They need love for the world and peace for the world.

They need fairness in the rule of their trade and in using

the intellectual rights. I mean, they easily steal the wisdom of other countries, technologies or things like that. So, they must be fair in the near future. That is the standpoint of a great country. They must be changed. They must be educated. I already started to change the world.

OIKAWA

I think you are right, but I still didn't understand why the past U.S. presidents didn't take that strategy against China.

TRUMP'S G.S.

Because they are weak people. I'm not so weak. I, myself, feel that I can hear the thinking or emotion of God. So, I'm the representative of God. I think so.

Mr. Ryuho Okawa made a path to the future, so I will just run through this way. We, I mean the U.S. and Japan, Donald Trump and Ryuho Okawa, are the best alliances of the world. We can make, remake the new world.

The North Korean problem is not more than a hurricane. It's OK. I will deal with it and I'll settle it. You can rely on us.

Nuclear armament of Japan? "It's OK"

ICHIKAWA

What do you think about the nuclear armament of Japan?

TRUMP'S G.S.

Hmm? It's OK. If you want, it's OK, of course. Please use your money, if possible. Or, you can make a lease from the U.S. and pay money to us. It's easy for you. I'll lend you nuclear weapons. [*Laughs.*]

AYAORI

Can I return to the subject of ICBM? Do the ICBMs you are planning to use contain nuclear missiles?

TRUMP'S G.S.

Of course.

AYAORI

Of course?

TRUMP'S G.S.

Of course. They already contain nuclear missiles. It's just my judgment. If I say "Go!" they will die.

When and how will Kim Jong-un be killed?

OIKAWA

But still, it sounds difficult to find the real place where Kim Jong-un is hiding. Maybe deep inside, under the earth. How will you find him?

TRUMP'S G.S.

It's a secret.

OIKAWA

I know.

TRUMP'S G.S.

We know where he is.

OIKAWA

OK. I know it's top-secret, but we, Japan, are the most important ally. That's why we would like to know, you already know how to find him?

TRUMP'S G.S.

[*Approximately 5 seconds of silence.*] Where there is a missile site and the next missile drill, there he will be. So, we can attack them.

OIKAWA

I see. So, once you attack him and kill him, you can experiment who he is by DNA test or something.

TRUMP'S G.S.

OK. If he has 50 or 60 replacements, we will kill all of them. No problem.

OIKAWA

So, finally, you will kill all people?

TRUMP'S G.S.

Yeah. All the people who say, "I am Kim Jong-un," anybody who says, "I am Kim Jong-un" will perish. That person's life.

OIKAWA

So, you believe you can justify that the United States can use nuclear weapons?

TRUMP'S G.S.

Of course, of course. We can use, we must use, and we will use nuclear weapons of ICBM. That is the best way. If we decide to use an ICBM, or 100 of ICBMs on North Korea, their one choice is to surrender. Just surrender. Next is perishment.

OIKAWA

Before you use nuclear weapons, will you announce to North Korea to recommend them to surrender?

TRUMP'S G.S.

It's top-secret. I'm sorry.

OIKAWA

OK.

ICHIKAWA

If they surrender, do you maintain...

TRUMP'S G.S.

He can surrender before I decide to launch the ICBMs.

ICHIKAWA

So, for your final decision, what is the last trigger to start the final action from the U.S.?

TRUMP'S G.S.

Next nuclear test.

ICHIKAWA

Ah. So, the next nuclear test will be the final trigger...

TRUMP'S G.S.

Yeah.

ICHIKAWA

...for you to start the final action? I see. OK.

TRUMP'S G.S.

[*Approximately 5 seconds of silence.*] They cannot survive.

Why did he mention liberty in the Speech before the Independence Day?

OIKAWA

Mr. President. Today, we really appreciate your comment.

TRUMP'S G.S.

You are a good man.

OIKAWA

And we really expect you to do the right thing under God's Will. You can save the people.

TRUMP'S G.S.

Please say hello to CNN.

[*Interviewers smile wryly.*]

OIKAWA

By the way, did you know that at the beginning of this month, Master Ryuho Okawa made a big speech in Tokyo Dome and that he talked about you?

TRUMP'S G.S.

Ah, really? Hmm.

OIKAWA

You didn't know that?

TRUMP'S G.S.

He's a good man. Every time, he says something good to me. It's OK. It will increase the reliance on Japan. It's a good religion. I wish you become greater and greater. You must be the next national religion.

AYAORI

In the speech before the Independence Day, you said "liberty comes from our Creator." Those words were very, very impressive. What is your thought on the Creator?

TRUMP'S G.S.

Ah, yeah. Recently, I've heard that the god of North America, whose name is Thoth or Toth*, like that, is the same soul of El Cantare, you said? So, our gods are the same. So, no problem.

AYAORI

I understand. Thank you.

TRUMP'S G.S.

And I know El Cantare is greater than Jesus Christ because in my running for the presidency, He, I mean El Cantare, defeated Hillary Clinton. Thank you very much for that.

OIKAWA

OK. So, during your very busy time, you have to deal with many issues, but you came here and you gave us many wonderful comments. Thank you so much. And we hope God blesses you.

TRUMP'S G.S.

And I want to say one thing to North Korean people. "Next

---

* Thoth is the god of wisdom in ancient Egyptian mythology. At Happy Science, it is said that Thoth was a great spiritual leader that built the golden age of the Atlantis civilization around 12,000 years ago. It has been revealed that he is the branch spirit of the God of Earth, El Cantare [refer to *The Laws of the Sun* and *The Nine Dimensions* (New York: IRH Press, 2018 and 2011, respectively)].

hurricane will fly to your country. It will come in the near future. Be careful about that."

OIKAWA

OK. Thank you so much.

Epilogue

Trump is Attempting to Pull Off An Amazing Move

What Kim Jong-un is aiming for is
A Yukimura Sanada-style surprise attack strategy

RYUHO OKAWA

[*Claps three times.*] Well, there we have it. [The guardian spirit of] Mr. Kim Jong-un knows that their power is very weak. So, just as the name came up earlier, he aims to be like Yukimura Sanada or Masashige Kusunoki [a Japanese military commander and samurai, respected for his exceptional military strategic skills]. You can see from his words here that he apparently thinks, if his "castle" is besieged and he is attacked, he will mount surprise attacks on his enemies, such as dropping stones from above, throwing feces and urine, or scattering oil.

AYAORI

Yes. I see.

President Trump's plan is "surrender or die"

RYUHO OKAWA

Meanwhile, President Trump's guardian spirit took the opposite approach of ignoring the manipulative techniques which said, "We'll sink your aircraft carriers," "We'll drop your fighters and bombers," or "We'll take the island." He is apparently thinking that North Korea will not surrender unless he comes out with a threat on the level of something like, "If war starts, we'll fire about one hundred ICBMs on you. You'll all be dead. If you survive after all of that, then you're lucky, but it may be inevitable that you all die. We would not be able to avoid around 20 million deaths. I'd rather have you dead than to have millions of people in other countries die."

That is to say, the "surrender or die" threat is the basic American strategy. They can't afford to waste their time on a fruitless, drawn-out battle.

AYAORI
Right.

RYUHO OKAWA
He is not planning on doing something so small as sending an Aegis ship there and dropping projectiles.

AYAORI
So, that is what he meant when he said, "Fury like the world has never seen."

RYUHO OKAWA
You know, we are lucky that he took over from President Obama. This will never end unless the U.S. threatens them on that level.

Japan must take action quickly with a Simple strategy such as an all-or-nothing plan

RYUHO OKAWA

However, North Korea still will not stop nuclear development, and if we keep putting this off saying, "We want peace" like Obama did, they will end up being fully equipped. If that happens, while the U.S. won't be demolished, Japan will.

AYAORI

Yes.

RYUHO OKAWA

If Japan were attacked with several dozen nuclear weapons, that would be the end of Japan. There really is no way to counter that, so if something is not done soon, it will be too late. Thus, I think we should fight with a simple strategy such as an all-or-nothing plan. Also, if the U.S. meets them with this level of attitude, Russia and China would not be able to do anything, either.

AYAORI

That is true.

RYUHO OKAWA

If the U.S. tries to move in a too complicated way, they would probably be met with all sorts of tricks. But if the U.S. comes at them like a top sumo wrestler throwing his real physical weight forward, I think Russia and China will only be able to watch with their hands tied. I really do think there is some sort of meaning behind President Trump appearing on the stage.

North Korea has no way of intercepting ICBMs

RYUHO OKAWA

As I said at the Tokyo Dome lecture [a grand lecture titled, "The Choice of Humankind" given on August 2, 2017], what I want from North Korea is for them to surrender. After all, when there is no possibility of winning, giving up is one of the responsibilities of a leader. If there is absolutely no possibility of winning, you must give up. Saying, "I might die, but I don't care if I am executed as long as my citizens are spared," is how a leader should be.

There is no way they could win fighting against the U.S. I think the only thing North Korea could do is to see how many South Koreans and Japanese people they could take down with them. However, if they have such petty thoughts, they would fall to Hell after death and never be able to escape from there. They could only become devils forever. So, I really do want them to stop this foolish line of thought.

AYAORI

I see.

RYUHO OKAWA

The most frightening thing to North Korea is that they will not be able to intercept American ICBMs. If the attacks from the U.S. are small, then they are ready to fight against anything that comes at them. For example, I imagine they are thinking things like, "If conventional missiles are fired at us, we will fire back with artillery shells." But if ballistic missiles are dropped smack down on them, there will be no way they can defend against that. If they are told, "We are going to wipe you all out in one swoop," they can do nothing. However, that timing might arise in the near future.

What the guardian spirit of President Trump referred to as top-secret information is something that could be related to that.

AYAORI

Yes.

RYUHO OKAWA

Mr. Trump probably thinks that there is a higher possibility of them surrendering if he shows them real anger. I think he feels, "We won't be able to settle this if we are all frightened merely over threats to Guam." Or, just like the Filipino President Duterte, acting crazy in order to scare people might be a good strategy.

AYAORI

[*Laughs.*]

RYUHO OKAWA

A "nice" person would not be fitting. A nice person gives too much latitude over a long period of time and ends up getting dragged along. The South Korean president is a populist and tries to look good all the time, but if talks stretch out for too long because of this, North Korea would complete their preparations during that time. If they come out and say, "OK, we have finished preparing our nuclear weapons," then everything would be over.

What Kennedy did against the USSR, One of the strongest powers at the time, During the Cuban Missile Crisis

RYUHO OKAWA

In any case, the intuition of a risk-taker like me says that the time for a decision is near. And I think this is the reason Mr. Trump appeared. Even in the case of the USSR, when Kennedy made up his mind firmly and said, "If you do not withdraw your nuclear missiles from Cuba, we will not back down from a full scale war," Khrushchev pulled them all out and cowered back home.

However, compared to the USSR, North Korea is very weak. The USSR at that time was almost the strongest power in the world. In fact, it was an era of hegemonic competition in which the U.S. and the USSR were competing for the strongest. Conversely, North Korea is not even at a level where it can compete for hegemony. In terms of Japan, for instance, it is as if the poorest prefecture is trying to put up a fight. It is no match. I imagine that the budget of the Japan Self-Defense Forces is about the same as the entire national budget of North Korea.

AYAORI

North Korea might even be smaller than that.

RYUHO OKAWA

Yes, that is true. They are definitely not at the level of contesting hegemony. It's as if a gofer serving a gangster is trying to come off as threatening. I think North Korea feels they won't be able to fight if their backup were to go away.

AYAORI

Yes.

RYUHO OKAWA

Thus, I think Kim Jong-un at least needs to be prepared to learn from the old Japanese army and sacrifice his own life if he feels like there is no way he can win. If he does that, it will end. At least one person might need to die, but after he dies, everyone else can be spared. Even if this allows North Korea to be absorbed into South Korea, the citizens would not have to face any sort of trouble at all.

Of course, I think we would have to take away all of the nuclear weapons and missiles and sink them in the ocean, though.

AYAORI

Yes.

In order to protect human rights, It is necessary to be as intimidating as to Ignore human rights

RYUHO OKAWA

In any case, Kim Jong-un is taking a big gamble, but he picked the wrong person. He probably should have fought when Obama was in office instead. I do not think he can win against Mr. Trump.

Mr. Trump is very strong. He might have a bad reputation within his own country right now, but to be tossed about by the mass media would mean to be weak against the left wing [as previous presidents were]. Mr. Trump is not like that. To be as intimidating as to ignore human rights might be a better way to protect human rights.

AYAORI
Right.

RYUHO OKAWA
If we roll back the clock to last year, looking at Mr. Obama, he went to Hiroshima and spoke of "a world without nuclear weapons." Also, Mr. Abe laid out the flattery and said the same kinds of things, speaking of "the power of reconciliation." However, Kim Jong-un is not someone we could ever hope to win against with that attitude. He has absolutely no intention of reconciliation, so that road is simply useless.

So, yes, I want the U.S. to use their superior strength and push the opponent out of the ring with "one blow" as a *yokozuna*. I think to show such kind of resolution has more potential to actually end the conflict without spilling blood. It is important to show our determination.

AYAORI
We will let everyone know.

You must not come out weak
Against the criminal type of people

RYUHO OKAWA

Mr. Duterte is also intimidating. He has had drug dealers come out and turn themselves in out of the fear that he actually kills dealers. In fact, there have been so many people that the jails are overflowing. When Duterte said something like, "In order to eliminate the four million drug addicts, be ready to kill anyone who resists. Either you all kill me, or I will kill you all," many people came out to turn themselves in. In this way, I think everyone should be aware that you must not come out too weak against the criminal type of people.

In any case, I want to see this resolved. If the idea is to draw this out and think that it's peaceful as long as nothing happens, I believe Japan will be at more and more of a disadvantage. North Korea most likely has several dozen nuclear warheads ready. If this number increases to several hundred, we won't be able to do anything against them.

If the U.S. adopts a way of minimizing damages by precision bombing, I think it will grow into a very difficult negotiation. However, if the U.S. is resolved to demolish the entire nation, North Korea will have no way out. They are even saying, "We will hit Trump Tower," so we have to be resolute enough to say such a thing back at them. I pray that

The Liberty [a monthly magazine issued by Happy Science] will do good work.

AYAORI

Right, we will do our best. Thank you very much.

ABOUT THE AUTHOR

Founder and CEO of Happy Science Group.

Ryuho Okawa was born on July 7th 1956, in Tokushima, Japan. After graduating from the University of Tokyo with a law degree, he joined a Tokyo-based trading house. While working at its New York headquarters, he studied international finance at the Graduate Center of the City University of New York. In 1981, he attained Great Enlightenment and became aware that he is El Cantare with a mission to bring salvation to all humankind.

In 1986, he established Happy Science. It now has members in over 166 countries across the world, with more than 700 branches and temples as well as 10,000 missionary houses around the world.

He has given over 3,450 lectures (of which more than 150 are in English) and published over 3,100 books (of which more than 600 are Spiritual Interview Series), and many are translated into 41 languages. Along with *The Laws of the Sun* and *The Laws Of Messiah*, many of the books have become best sellers or million sellers. To date, Happy Science has produced 26 movies. The original story and original concept were given by the Executive Producer Ryuho Okawa. He has also composed music and written lyrics of over 450 pieces.

Moreover, he is the Founder of Happy Science University and Happy Science Academy (Junior and Senior High School), Founder and President of the Happiness Realization Party, Founder and Honorary Headmaster of Happy Science Institute of Government and Management, Founder of IRH Press Co., Ltd., and the Chairperson of NEW STAR PRODUCTION Co., Ltd. and ARI Production Co., Ltd.

WHAT IS EL CANTARE?

El Cantare means "the Light of the Earth," and is the Supreme God of the Earth who has been guiding humankind since the beginning of Genesis. He is whom Jesus called Father and Muhammad called Allah, and is *Ame-no-Mioya-Gami*, Japanese Father God. Different parts of El Cantare's core consciousness have descended to Earth in the past, once as Alpha and another as Elohim. His branch spirits, such as Shakyamuni Buddha and Hermes, have descended to Earth many times and helped to flourish many civilizations. To unite various religions and to integrate various fields of study in order to build a new civilization on Earth, a part of the core consciousness has descended to Earth as Master Ryuho Okawa.

Alpha is a part of the core consciousness of El Cantare who descended to Earth around 330 million years ago. Alpha preached Earth's Truths to harmonize and unify Earth-born humans and space people who came from other planets.

Elohim is a part of El Cantare's core consciousness who descended to Earth around 150 million years ago. He gave wisdom, mainly on the differences of light and darkness, good and evil.

Ame-no-Mioya-Gami (Japanese Father God) is the Creator God and the Father God who appears in the ancient literature, *Hotsuma Tsutae*. It is believed that He descended on the foothills of Mt. Fuji about 30,000 years ago and built the Fuji dynasty, which is the root of the Japanese civilization. With justice as the central pillar, Ame-no-Mioya-Gami's teachings spread to ancient civilizations of other countries in the world.

Shakyamuni Buddha was born as a prince into the Shakya Clan in India around 2,600 years ago. When he was 29 years old, he renounced the world and sought enlightenment. He later attained Great Enlightenment and founded Buddhism.

Hermes is one of the 12 Olympian gods in Greek mythology, but the spiritual Truth is that he taught the teachings of love and progress around 4,300 years ago that became the origin of the current Western civilization. He is a hero that truly existed.

Ophealis was born in Greece around 6,500 years ago and was the leader who took an expedition to as far as Egypt. He is the God of miracles, prosperity, and arts, and is known as Osiris in the Egyptian mythology.

Rient Arl Croud was born as a king of the ancient Incan Empire around 7,000 years ago and taught about the mysteries of the mind. In the heavenly world, he is responsible for the interactions that take place between various planets.

Thoth was an almighty leader who built the golden age of the Atlantic civilization around 12,000 years ago. In the Egyptian mythology, he is known as god Thoth.

Ra Mu was a leader who built the golden age of the civilization of Mu around 17,000 years ago. As a religious leader and a politician, he ruled by uniting religion and politics.

WHAT IS A SPIRITUAL MESSAGE?

We are all spiritual beings living on this earth. The following is the mechanism behind Master Ryuho Okawa's spiritual messages.

1 You are a spirit

People are born into this world to gain wisdom through various experiences and return to the other world when their lives end. We are all spirits and repeat this cycle in order to refine our souls.

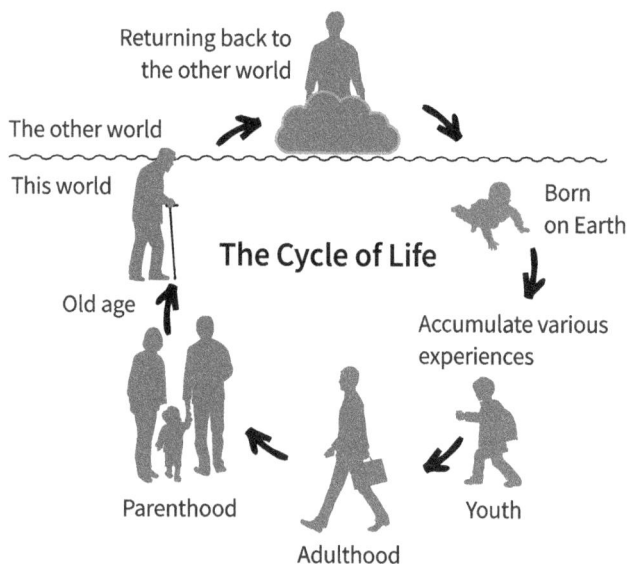

Returning back to
the other world

The other world

This world

Born
on Earth

The Cycle of Life

Old age

Accumulate various
experiences

Parenthood

Youth

Adulthood

2 You have a guardian spirit

Guardian spirits are those who protect the people who are living on this earth. Each of us has a guardian spirit that watches over us and guides us from the other world. They were us in our past life, and are identical in how we think.

3 How spiritual messages work

Master Ryuho Okawa, through his enlightenment, is capable of summoning any spirit from anywhere in the world, including the spirit world.

Master Okawa's way of receiving spiritual messages is fundamentally different from that of other psychic mediums who undergo trances and are thereby completely taken over by the spirits they are channeling.

Master Okawa's attainment of a high level of enlightenment enables him to retain full control of his consciousness and body throughout the duration of the spiritual message. To allow the spirits to express their own thoughts and personalities freely, however, Master Okawa usually softens the dominancy of his consciousness. This way, he is able to keep his own philosophies out of the way and ensure that the spiritual messages are pure expressions of the spirits he is channeling.

Since guardian spirits think at the same subconscious level as the person living on earth, Master Okawa can summon the spirit and find out what the person on earth is actually thinking. If the person has already returned to the other world, the spirit can give messages to the people living on earth through Master Okawa.

Since 2009, many spiritual messages have been openly recorded by Master Okawa and published. Spiritual messages from the guardian spirits of people living today such as Donald Trump, former Japanese Prime Minister Shinzo Abe and Chinese President Xi Jinping, as well as spiritual messages sent from the spirit world by Jesus Christ, Muhammad, Thomas Edison, Mother Teresa, Steve Jobs and Nelson Mandela are just a tiny pack of spiritual messages that were published so far.

Domestically, in Japan, these spiritual messages are being read by a wide range of politicians and mass media, and the high-level contents of these books are delivering an impact even more on politics, news and public opinion. In recent years, there have been spiritual messages recorded in English, and

English translations are being done on the spiritual messages given in Japanese. These have been published overseas, one after another, and have started to shake the world.

1. The guardian spirit / spirit in the other world...

2. Goes inside Master Okawa in this world

3. Master Okawa speaks the words of the guardian spirit / spirit

For more about spiritual messages and a complete list of books in the Spiritual Interview Series, visit okawabooks.com

ABOUT HAPPY SCIENCE

Happy Science is a global movement that empowers individuals to find purpose and spiritual happiness and to share that happiness with their families, societies, and the world. With more than 12 million members around the world, Happy Science aims to increase awareness of spiritual truths and expand our capacity for love, compassion, and joy so that together we can create the kind of world we all wish to live in.

Activities at Happy Science are based on the Principle of Happiness (Love, Wisdom, Self-Reflection, and Progress). This principle embraces worldwide philosophies and beliefs, transcending boundaries of culture and religions.

Love teaches us to give ourselves freely without expecting anything in return; it encompasses giving, nurturing, and forgiving.

Wisdom leads us to the insights of spiritual truths, and opens us to the true meaning of life and the will of God (the universe, the highest power, Buddha).

Self-Reflection brings a mindful, nonjudgmental lens to our thoughts and actions to help us find our truest selves—the essence of our souls—and deepen our connection to the highest power. It helps us attain a clean and peaceful mind and leads us to the right life path.

Progress emphasizes the positive, dynamic aspects of our spiritual growth—actions we can take to manifest and spread happiness around the world. It's a path that not only expands our soul growth, but also furthers the collective potential of the world we live in.

PROGRAMS AND EVENTS

The doors of Happy Science are open to all. We offer a variety of programs and events, including self-exploration and self-growth programs, spiritual seminars, meditation and contemplation sessions, study groups, and book events.

Our programs are designed to:
* Deepen your understanding of your purpose and meaning in life
* Improve your relationships and increase your capacity to love unconditionally
* Attain peace of mind, decrease anxiety and stress, and feel positive
* Gain deeper insights and a broader perspective on the world
* Learn how to overcome life's challenges
  ... and much more.

For more information, visit happy-science.org.

OUR ACTIVITIES

Happy Science does other various activities to provide support for those in need.

◆ **You Are An Angel! General Incorporated Association**
Happy Science has a volunteer network in Japan that encourages and supports children with disabilities as well as their parents and guardians.

◆ **Never Mind School for Truancy**
At 'Never Mind,' we support students who find it very challenging to attend schools in Japan. We also nurture their self-help spirit and power to rebound against obstacles in life based on Master Okawa's teachings and faith.

◆ **"Prevention Against Suicide" Campaign since 2003**
A nationwide campaign to reduce suicides; over 20,000 people commit suicide every year in Japan. "The Suicide Prevention Website-Words of Truth for You-" presents spiritual prescriptions for worries such as depression, lost love, extramarital affairs, bullying and work-related problems, thereby saving many lives.

◆ **Support for Anti-bullying Campaigns**
Happy Science provides support for a group of parents and guardians, Network to Protect Children from Bullying, a general incorporated foundation launched in Japan to end bullying, including those that can even be called a criminal offense. So far, the network received more than 5,000 cases and resolved 90% of them.

- **The Golden Age Scholarship**

  This scholarship is granted to students who can contribute greatly and bring a hopeful future to the world.

- **Success No.1**
  Buddha's Truth Afterschool Academy

  Happy Science has over 180 classrooms throughout Japan and in several cities around the world that focus on afterschool education for children. The education focuses on faith and morals in addition to supporting children's school studies.

- **Angel Plan V**

  For children under the age of kindergarten, Happy Science holds classes for nurturing healthy, positive, and creative boys and girls.

- **Future Stars Training Department**

  The Future Stars Training Department was founded within the Happy Science Media Division with the goal of nurturing talented individuals to become successful in the performing arts and entertainment industry.

- **NEW STAR PRODUCTION Co., Ltd.**
  ARI Production Co., Ltd.

  We have companies to nurture actors and actresses, artists, and vocalists. They are also involved in film production.

CONTACT INFORMATION

Happy Science is a worldwide organization with branches and temples around the globe. For a comprehensive list, visit the worldwide directory at *happy-science.org*. The following are some of the many Happy Science locations:

UNITED STATES AND CANADA

New York
79 Franklin St., New York, NY 10013, USA
Phone: 1-212-343-7972
Fax: 1-212-343-7973
Email: ny@happy-science.org
Website: happyscience-usa.org

New Jersey
66 Hudson St., #2R, Hoboken, NJ 07030, USA
Phone: 1-201-313-0127
Email: nj@happy-science.org
Website: happyscience-usa.org

Chicago
2300 Barrington Rd., Suite #400,
Hoffman Estates, IL 60169, USA
Phone: 1-630-937-3077
Email: chicago@happy-science.org
Website: happyscience-usa.org

Florida
5208 8th St., Zephyrhills, FL 33542, USA
Phone: 1-813-715-0000
Fax: 1-813-715-0010
Email: florida@happy-science.org
Website: happyscience-usa.org

Atlanta
1874 Piedmont Ave., NE Suite 360-C
Atlanta, GA 30324, USA
Phone: 1-404-892-7770
Email: atlanta@happy-science.org
Website: happyscience-usa.org

San Francisco
525 Clinton St.
Redwood City, CA 94062, USA
Phone & Fax: 1-650-363-2777
Email: sf@happy-science.org
Website: happyscience-usa.org

Los Angeles
1590 E. Del Mar Blvd., Pasadena, CA
91106, USA
Phone: 1-626-395-7775
Fax: 1-626-395-7776
Email: la@happy-science.org
Website: happyscience-usa.org

Orange County
16541 Gothard St. Suite 104
Huntington Beach, CA 92647
Phone: 1-714-659-1501
Email: oc@happy-science.org
Website: happyscience-usa.org

San Diego
7841 Balboa Ave. Suite #202
San Diego, CA 92111, USA
Phone: 1-626-395-7775
Fax: 1-626-395-7776
E-mail: sandiego@happy-science.org
Website: happyscience-usa.org

Hawaii
Phone: 1-808-591-9772
Fax: 1-808-591-9776
Email: hi@happy-science.org
Website: happyscience-usa.org

Kauai
3343 Kanakolu Street, Suite 5
Lihue, HI 96766, USA
Phone: 1-808-822-7007
Fax: 1-808-822-6007
Email: kauai-hi@happy-science.org
Website: happyscience-usa.org

Toronto

845 The Queensway
Etobicoke, ON M8Z 1N6, Canada
Phone: 1-416-901-3747
Email: toronto@happy-science.org
Website: happy-science.ca

Vancouver

#201-2607 East 49th Avenue,
Vancouver, BC, V5S 1J9, Canada
Phone: 1-604-437-7735
Fax: 1-604-437-7764
Email: vancouver@happy-science.org
Website: happy-science.ca

INTERNATIONAL

Tokyo

1-6-7 Togoshi, Shinagawa,
Tokyo, 142-0041, Japan
Phone: 81-3-6384-5770
Fax: 81-3-6384-5776
Email: tokyo@happy-science.org
Website: happy-science.org

Seoul

74, Sadang-ro 27-gil,
Dongjak-gu, Seoul, Korea
Phone: 82-2-3478-8777
Fax: 82-2-3478-9777
Email: korea@happy-science.org
Website: happyscience-korea.org

London

3 Margaret St.
London, W1W 8RE United Kingdom
Phone: 44-20-7323-9255
Fax: 44-20-7323-9344
Email: eu@happy-science.org
Website: www.happyscience-uk.org

Taipei

No. 89, Lane 155, Dunhua N. Road,
Songshan District, Taipei City 105, Taiwan
Phone: 886-2-2719-9377
Fax: 886-2-2719-5570
Email: taiwan@happy-science.org
Website: happyscience-tw.org

Sydney

516 Pacific Highway, Lane Cove North,
2066 NSW, Australia
Phone: 61-2-9411-2877
Fax: 61-2-9411-2822
Email: sydney@happy-science.org

Kuala Lumpur

No 22A, Block 2, Jalil Link Jalan Jalil
Jaya 2, Bukit Jalil 57000,
Kuala Lumpur, Malaysia
Phone: 60-3-8998-7877
Fax: 60-3-8998-7977
Email: malaysia@happy-science.org
Website: happyscience.org.my

Sao Paulo

Rua. Domingos de Morais 1154,
Vila Mariana, Sao Paulo SP
CEP 04010-100, Brazil
Phone: 55-11-5088-3800
Email: sp@happy-science.org
Website: happyscience.com.br

Kathmandu

Kathmandu Metropolitan City,
Ward No. 15, Ring Road, Kimdol,
Sitapaila Kathmandu, Nepal
Phone: 977-1-427-2931
Email: nepal@happy-science.org

Jundiai

Rua Congo, 447, Jd. Bonfiglioli
Jundiai-CEP, 13207-340, Brazil
Phone: 55-11-4587-5952
Email: jundiai@happy-science.org

Kampala

Plot 877 Rubaga Road, Kampala
P.O. Box 34130 Kampala, UGANDA
Email: uganda@happy-science.org

ABOUT HAPPINESS REALIZATION PARTY

The Happiness Realization Party (HRP) was founded in May 2009 by Master Ryuho Okawa as part of the Happy Science Group. HRP strives to improve the Japanese society, based on three basic political principles of "freedom, democracy, and faith," and let Japan promote individual and public happiness from Asia to the world as a leader nation.

1) Diplomacy and Security: Protecting Freedom, Democracy, and Faith of Japan and the World from China's Totalitarianism

Japan's current defense system is insufficient against China's expanding hegemony and the threat of North Korea's nuclear missiles. Japan, as the leader of Asia, must strengthen its defense power and promote strategic diplomacy together with the nations which share the values of freedom, democracy, and faith. Further, HRP aims to realize world peace under the leadership of Japan, the nation with the spirit of religious tolerance.

2) Economy: Early economic recovery through utilizing the "wisdom of the private sector"

Economy has been damaged severely by the novel coronavirus originated in China. Many companies have been forced into bankruptcy or out of business. What is needed for economic recovery now is not subsidies and regulations by the government, but policies which can utilize the "wisdom of the private sector."

For more information, visit en.hr-party.jp

HAPPY SCIENCE ACADEMY
JUNIOR AND SENIOR HIGH SCHOOL

Happy Science Academy Junior and Senior High School is a boarding school founded with the goal of educating the future leaders of the world who can have a big vision, persevere, and take on new challenges.

Currently, there are two campuses in Japan; the Nasu Main Campus in Tochigi Prefecture, founded in 2010, and the Kansai Campus in Shiga Prefecture, founded in 2013.

Nasu Main Campus

Kansai Campus

H⳥ᵤ HAPPY SCIENCE UNIVERSITY

THE FOUNDING SPIRIT AND THE GOAL OF EDUCATION

Based on the founding philosophy of the university, "Exploration of happiness and the creation of a new civilization," education, research and studies will be provided to help students acquire deep understanding grounded in religious belief and advanced expertise with the objectives of producing "great talents of virtue" who can contribute in a broad-ranging way to serve Japan and the international society.

FACULTIES

Faculty of human happiness

Students in this faculty will pursue liberal arts from various perspectives with a multidisciplinary approach, explore and envision an ideal state of human beings and society.

Faculty of successful management

This faculty aims to realize successful management that helps organizations to create value and wealth for society and to contribute to the happiness and the development of management and employees as well as society as a whole.

Faculty of future creation

Students in this faculty study subjects such as political science, journalism, performing arts and artistic expression, and explore and present new political and cultural models based on truth, goodness and beauty.

Faculty of future industry

This faculty aims to nurture engineers who can resolve various issues facing modern civilization from a technological standpoint and contribute to the creation of new industries of the future.

ABOUT HS PRESS

HS Press is an imprint of IRH Press Co., Ltd. IRH Press Co., Ltd., based in Tokyo, was founded in 1987 as a publishing division of Happy Science. IRH Press publishes religious and spiritual books, journals, magazines and also operates broadcast and film production enterprises. For more information, visit *okawabooks.com*.

Follow us on:

f Facebook: Okawa Books   Instagram: OkawaBooks

Youtube: Okawa Books   Twitter: Okawa Books

Pinterest: Okawa Books   g Goodreads: Ryuho Okawa

--- **NEWSLETTER** ---

To receive book related news, promotions and events, please subscribe to our newsletter below.

∞ eepurl.com/bsMeJj

--- **AUDIO / VISUAL MEDIA** ---

YOUTUBE

PODCAST

Introduction of Ryuho Okawa's titles; topics ranging from self-help, current affairs, spirituality, religion, and the universe.

BOOKS BY RYUHO OKAWA

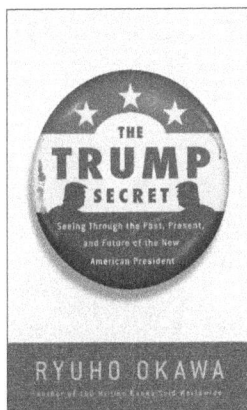

THE TRUMP SECRET
SEEING THROUGH THE PAST, PRESENT, AND FUTURE OF THE NEW AMERICAN PRESIDENT

Donald Trump's victory in the 2016 presidential election surprised almost all major vote forecasters who predicted Hillary Clinton's victory. But 10 months earlier, in January 2016, Ryuho Okawa, Global Visionary, a renowned spiritual leader, and international best-selling author, had already foreseen Trump's victory. This book contains a series of lectures and interviews that unveil the secrets to Trump's victory and makes predictions of what will happen under his presidency. This book predicts the coming of a new America that will go through a great transformation from the "red and blue states" to the United States.

Contents

Chapter 1: On Victory of Mr. Donald Trump

Chapter 2: Freedom, Justice, and Happiness

Chapter 3: Spiritual Interview with George Washington

Chapter 4: The Trump Card in the United States

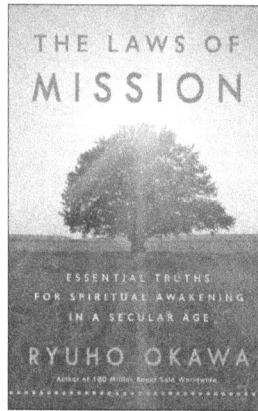

THE LAWS OF MISSION

ESSENTIAL TRUTHS FOR SPIRITUAL AWAKENING IN A SECULAR AGE

What do people live for?
Where do they come from, and where do they go after death?

Your unforgettable failures in the past.
Your worries and sufferings in the present.
Your anxieties about the future.
Live according to the book, and you'll resolve all of the above!

Here's the answer key to your questions in life.

the Laws of
JUSTICE

How We Can Solve World Conflict & Bring Peace

How can we resolve conflicts in this world? There are two major trends opposing each other in the world today. One centers around the United States. This force is comprised of countries that want to support and spread the ideologies of democracy, liberalism, fundamental human rights and market economics. The other is a force comprised of countries that will suffer if these ideologies spread across the world, because their ways of thinking and methods differ. There is a battle between these two forces. *[continued inside]*

RYUHO OKAWA
Author of 100 Million Books Sold Worldwide

THE LAWS OF JUSTICE
HOW WE CAN SOLVE
WORLD CONFLICTS & BRING PEACE

How can we solve conflicts in this world? Why is it that we continue to live in a world of turmoil, when we all wish to live in a world of peace and harmony?

In recent years, we've faced issues that jeopardize international peace and security, including the rise of ISIS, Syrian civil war and refugee crisis, break-off of diplomatic relations between Saudi Arabia and Iran, Russia's annexation of Crimea, China's military expansion, and North Korea's nuclear development.

This book shows what global justice is from a comprehensive perspective of the Supreme God. Becoming aware of this view will let us embrace differences in beliefs, recognize other people's divine nature, and love and forgive one another. It will also become the key to solving the issues we face, whether they're religious, political, societal, economic, or academic, and help the world become a better and safer world for all of us living today.

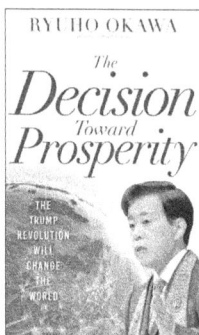

THE DECISION TOWARD PROSPERITY

THE TRUMP REVOLUTION WILL CHANGE THE WORLD

In the book, Okawa talks a lot about Japanese politics as Japan is his mother country, but the universal philosophy behind his words will surely enlighten readers in other countries too. This is the guidebook that will help the world realize prosperity for the next 300 years.

INTO THE STORM OF INTERNATIONAL POLITICS

THE NEW STANDARDS OF THE WORLD ORDER

The world is now seeking a new idea or a new philosophy. In this book, Okawa presents new standards of the world order while giving his own analysis on world affairs concerning the U.S., China, Islamic State and others.

RYUHO OKAWA - A POLITICAL REVOLUTIONARY

THE ORIGINATOR OF ABENOMICS AND FATHER OF THE HAPPINESS REALIZATION PARTY

In this book, Okawa lays down the guiding principles and the ways to breakthrough on the topics of economy, finance, nuclear power plant, foreign diplomacy, social welfare, and society with aging population and a falling birth rate.

For a complete list of books, visit okawabooks.com

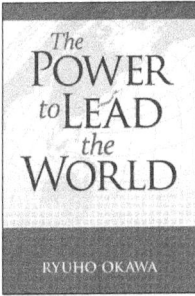

THE POWER TO LEAD THE WORLD

"It is not enough to speak only of ideals; we must envision how this world should be while setting our eyes firmly on things like real politics."

— Ryuho Okawa

[This book is available only in local branches and temples. Please refer to the contact information.]

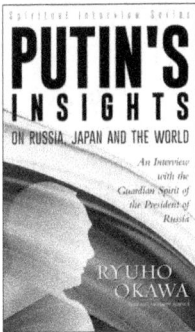

PUTIN'S INSIGHTS ON RUSSIA, JAPAN AND THE WORLD

AN INTERVIEW WITH THE GUARDIAN SPIRIT OF THE PRESIDENT OF RUSSIA

In this book, the guardian spirit of President Putin and asks his opinion on the current world leaders, how he looks upon Syrian affairs and the confusion in the EU, and on what he predicts will happen in the next 5 years with the Asian crisis.

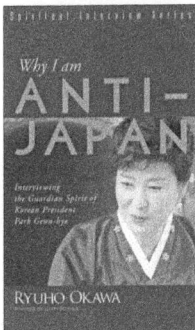

WHY I AM AMTI-JAPAN

INTERVIEWING THE GUARDIAN SPIRIT OF KOREAN PRESIDENT PARK GEUN-HYE

This book is the record of interviews conducted on President Park's subconscious [guardian spirit] in February 2014, which were done in order to find out the fundamental reason to her anti-Japanese sentiments. Her true thoughts, as well as the truth on modern Japan-Korea history, were revealed in these interviews.

For a complete list of books, visit okawabooks.com

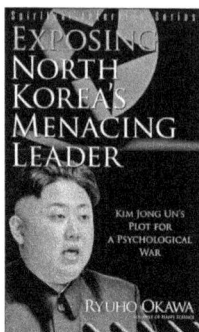

EXPOSING NORTH KOREA'S MENACING LEADER
KIM JONG UN'S PLOT FOR A PSYCHOLOGICAL WAR

This book reveals the role that North Korea is playing in China's imperialistic strategy and the two nations' close ties with Iran. Together, China and Kim Jong Un are carrying out a psychological war that takes full advantage of the weaknesses of Japanese Prime Minister Abe and United States President Obama.

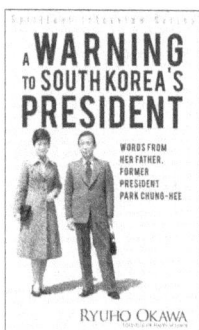

A WARNING TO SOUTH KOREA'S PRESIDENT
WORDS FROM HER FATHER, FORMER PRESIDENT PARK CHUNG-HEE

Chung-hee's spirit shares his opinions on the roles of South Korea, Japan, the United States, China, and North Korea in the global context. This interview lets us see history in a new light and shows us how to build a better future for the Asia-Pacific region.

SOUTH KOREA'S CONSPIRACY
PRESIDENT PARK'S HIDDEN AGENDA TO UNITE WITH CHINA

On June 27, 2013, South Korea's President Park Geun-hye and Chinese President Xi Jinping held summit talks in Beijing. Okawa hopes that these interviews will provide a truthful understanding of the historical events and help us understand the nature of true international justice.

For a complete list of books, visit okawabooks.com

Unmasking Ban Ki-Moon's Biased Stance

Investigating the Paralysis of the United Nations

In this spiritual interview with the guardian spirit of Mr. Ban Ki-moon, the U.N. Secretary-General's true character and true intentions regarding his important peacemaking responsibilities is revealed.

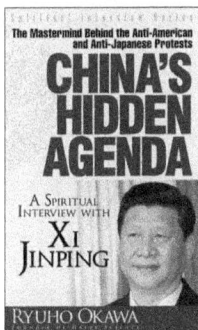

China's Hidden Agenda

The Mastermind Behind the Anti-American and Anti-Japanese Protests

"Anti-American demonstrations have been raging in over twenty Arab countries. The man pulling the strings behind all this is Xi Jinping."

— Ryuho Okawa

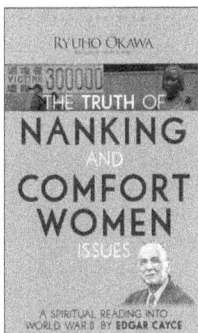

The Truth of Nanking and Comfort Women Issues

A Spiritual Reading into World War II by Edgar Cayce

Did the so-called "Nanking Massacre" and the military comfort women forcefully taken by the Japanese troops actually exist as historical facts? This book reviews the causes of World War II and reveal the true world history.

For a complete list of books, visit okawabooks.com

* 9 7 9 8 8 8 7 3 7 0 8 4 2 *